The Enneagram:

Its Source, History, Development and Meaning

by Joseph Lumpkin, Breandan Lumpkin, and Anne Burton

I wish to thank the following authors for their contributions to this work. Source materials used in this book are provided by permission of and collaboration with the following authors.

Enneagram: Finding Your Type and Making Sense of the System by Breandan Lumpkin, published by Fifth Estate, Inc. 2022, ISBN 979-8369874578

Numerology, A Book of Insights by Anne Burton, published by Fifth Estate, Inc. 2007, ISBN: 9781933580456

I would also like to thank Jude Novak. The head editor of this book.

Thank you for your assistance and insights.

Sincerely,

Joseph Lumpkin

Enneagram: Its Source, History, Development and Meaning

Copyright © 2023 by Joseph Lumpkin, Breandan Lumpkin, and Anne Burton

All rights reserved.

Printed in the United States of America. No part of this book may be used or reproduced in any manner whatsoever without written permission except in the case of brief quotations embodied in critical articles and reviews.

Fifth Estate Publishing, Blountsville, AL 35031

Printed on acid-free paper

ISBN: 9798375339146

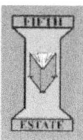

Fifth Estate, 2023

Table of Contents

Setting the Stage for Wisdom	7
The philosophy of Pythagoras	10
Letters Become Numbers	24
The Chaldean Approach	34
Vedic Numerology	44
Pythagorean Numerology	58
Bible Number Symbology	66
The Numbers of the Tribes of Israel	70
Sufis and the Mystic Numbers	96
Origins of the System	102
The Enneagram According to Oscar Ichazo	128
The Enneagram of Personality	144
Naranjo's Enneagram	150
A Comparison of Numerology and the Enneagram	154
Tips to Becoming a Better You	248
Conclusion	266

Setting the Stage for Wisdom

The Enneagram is a personality profiling system used to categorize people into nine distinct groups or types. The system has grown in popularity and spread from its beginnings in minds of mystics and sages to its use today as a tool in the hands of psychologists. The use of the Enneagram continues to grow as it has become popular among church ministers, counselors, and even the laity. The origins of the Enneagram are shrouded in mystery and historical ambiguity.

The Story of the Enneagram begins in the ancient nations of India, Egypt, Babylon, and Greece where esoteric knowledge of the human psyche was being developed. The story spans thousands of years and multiple nations as ancient teachings were transmitted and refined between gurus, priests, and philosophers. The knowledge was closely guarded by secret societies interested in finding the depth, breadth, and variegation present in the universe and in human personalities. These hidden reservoirs of knowledge were sought out and brought back together to form the basic structure of what is now called, The Enneagram.

This is the story of George Ivanovich Gurdjieff, the man credited with the idea and epiphany that became the Enneagram. This is the history of his wisdom-source. It is the story of how ancient and powerful insights of sages and holy men, long since dead, evolved to become the Enneagram of today.

The story crosses a distance of thousands of years and divergent views of the cosmos. It has been written time and time again in the pages of history as science is spawned from pseudo-science. Stories like this one reverberate and repeat in world history as astrology became astronomy and alchemy became chemistry, primitive cures were found to have scientific bases, and the myths were found to have historical facts. This time, the occult wisdom and insights into human nature and personality deemed sacred by Egyptians, Chaldeans, Jews, and Greeks are stripped of their occult vernier and applied directly to modern psychological techniques.

In this book, we will track the evolution of number symbology back through history, from hieroglyphs and letters to the numbers they became. We will divest numerology of its contrived formulae and meanings to reveal the jewel laying beneath. It is the diamond of understanding used by the founders of the Enneagram to facilitate its ability to encourage emotional and psychological growth toward a state of integration that C.G. Jung referred to as "Individuation".

As astrology laid aside its mystical meanings to reveal its pure mathematical genius, so has the Enneagram plumbed the underlying truth held within occult knowledge to reveal a way of defining, healing, and evolving personality types. Reliance on calculations based on a person's birthday or name is replaced by empirical data gathered through observation and proven tests. With this, a powerful and enlightening personality profiling system has been created from information once held by only mystics, Sufis, and philosophers for thousands of years.

We will trace and combine all major sources of numerology. Later, we will look at the places, nations, and regions visited by Gurdjieff and how he may have encountered this knowledge. Then, we will tie those secrets back to the modern Enneagram of today. Our theories will be proven by looking at a comparison of all major forms of numerology placed beside the personality types of the modern Enneagram.

We will start with the type of numerology most well-known and practiced, Pythagorean Numerology.

The Philosophy of Pythagoras

Pythagoras of Samos c. 570 – c. 495 BC) was an ancient Ionian Greek philosopher and the founder of Pythagoreanism. His political and religious teachings were well known throughout the region and were a powerful influence on the philosophies of Plato and Aristotle. Thus, through them, Pythagoras influenced the West.

He was the son of Mnesarchus, a gem-engraver on the island of Samos. Pythagoras had a thirst for knowledge and a burning belief in hidden, underlying principles behind the operation and laws of the cosmos. Owing to this, he traveled extensively in search of this knowledge.

Pythagoras received most of his education in the Near East. He studied in Egypt with priests and magi. Here, it is likely he came in contact with Chaldean Numerology, an older method of divination and possibly the first system to break people into personality types. Chaldean numerology was said to have originated in or near Chaldea, a small country that existed between the late 10th and mid-6th centuries BCE, located in the far southeastern corner of Mesopotamia. The Hebrew Bible uses the term כשדים and this is translated as Chaldean in the Greek Old Testament. The name is derived from a cognate of Kasdim, which refers to the south Mesopotamian people called the Kaldu. The Kaldu were the

West Semitic tribes of southern Babylonia mentioned in Assyrian texts written in the same period (10th - 6th centuries BCE). Around the 8th century BCE they began to lose their ethnic identity and were absorbed into the population of Babylonia. We will look into Chaldean numerology later as we compare various systems.

Pythagoras was well known in his own time, and thus mentioned in various texts. The writer Antiphon wrote during the Hellenistic Era. His work was used as a source by Porphyry. In the writing, *On Men of Outstanding Merit*, he claimed that Pythagoras learned to speak Egyptian from the Pharaoh Amasis II himself and that he studied with the Egyptian priests at Diospolis (Thebes). Pythagoras was the only foreigner ever to be granted the privilege of taking part in their worship. Ancient writers state Pythagoras learned geometry and the doctrine of metempsychosis from the Egyptians. Metempsychosis is the belief in transmigration of the soul. The belief holds that at death of the body the soul migrates into a new body of the same or a different species.

The Middle Platonist biographer Plutarch (c. 46 – c. 120 AD) writes in his treatise *On Isis and Osiris* that Pythagoras was taught by the priest Oenuphis of Heliopolis during his time in Eqypt. According to the Christian theologian Clement of Alexandria (c. 150 – c. 215 AD), "Pythagoras was a disciple of Soches, an Egyptian High-prophet, as well as Plato of Sechnuphis of Heliopolis." (Clement of Alexandria suggests that Plato traveled to Heliopolis and was a disciple of the Egyptian priest Sechnuphis.)

Other writers of the time claimed Pythagoras had learned much of his philosophy from the Magi in Persia. Others state he learned from Zoroaster himself. Diogenes Laërtius claimed that Pythagoras went to the Cave of Ida with Epimenides during his time in Crete. The Phoenicians allegedly taught Pythagoras arithmetic and the Chaldeans are said to have taught him astronomy. This claim further bolsters the fact that Pythagoras may have drawn his understanding of numbers from the earlier Chaldean sources.

Around 530 BCE, he traveled to Croton in southern Italy. There he founded a school, which was run more like a monastery, in which initiates were sworn to secrecy and lived a communal, ascetic lifestyle. This lifestyle included vegetarianism. The school, known as, "New Way of Life", was formed to pursue the religious and ascetic observances, and for studying religious and philosophical theories. The adherents were bound by a vow to Pythagoras and each other. The members of the sect shared all their possessions in common and were devoted to each other as well as to the exclusion of outsiders. The members of the sect vowed to devote themselves to one another and to isolate themselves from outsider. There was no individual ownership in the sect, instead all possessions were shared in common. Ancient sources record that the Pythagoreans ate meals in common after the manner of the Spartans. One Pythagorean maxim was "koinà tà phílōn" ("All things in common among friends").

Ancient writers, Iamblichus and Porphyry, provide detailed accounts of the school. Iamblichus presents Pythagoras's teachings as a pagan alternative to Christian monastic communities of his own time. It should be noted that various types of Gnosticism, a Christian sect, merged ideas and doctrine from Pythagoreanism and Christianity.

Two groups existed within early Pythagoreanism: the mathematikoi ("learners") and the akousmatikoi ("listeners"). The akousmatikoi are traditionally identified by scholars as "old believers" in mysticism, numerology, and religious teachings; whereas the mathematikoi are traditionally identified as a more intellectual, modernist faction who were more rationalist and scientific. Gregory cautions that there was probably not a sharp distinction between them and that many Pythagoreans probably believed the two approaches were compatible.

Pythagoreans study mathematics and music. They believed that music was a purification for the soul, just as medicine was a purification for the body. Pythagoras may have also devised the doctrine of musica universalis, which holds that the planets move according to mathematical equations and thus resonate to produce an inaudible symphony of music.

In antiquity, Pythagoras was credited with many mathematical and scientific discoveries, including the Pythagorean theorem, Pythagorean tuning of the musical scales, the idea that five solid shapes make up the universe, the Theory of Proportions, the idea that Earth is a sphere, and the identity of the morning and evening stars as the planet Venus. It was said that he was the first man to call himself a philosopher ("lover of wisdom") and that he was the first to divide the globe into five climatic zones.

The philosophy of Pythagoras was related to mathematics. It held that numbers were important and formed patterns on which nature rests. Pythagoreans believed that the principles of mathematics were the principles of all things. Pythagoras believed all things in the universe were created by and through numbers, thus all things could be expressed by numbers - qualified and quantified with numbers, including the human soul.

According to Pythagoras, all the planets are enclosed in a kind of transparent physical sphere, and there is a corresponding musical ratio with the distance between the planets.

Pythagorean ideas on mathematical perfection also impacted ancient Greek art. His teachings underwent a major revival in the first century BC among Middle Platonists, coinciding with the rise of Neopythagoreanism. Pythagoras continued to be regarded as a great philosopher throughout the Middle Ages and his philosophy had a major impact on scientists such as Nicolaus Copernicus, Johannes Kepler, and Isaac Newton. Pythagorean symbolism was used throughout early modern European esotericism. His teachings, as portrayed in Ovid's Metamorphoses, influenced the modern vegetarian movement. If one believes in the transmigration of the soul then one must take pause and consider all animal life equally sacred, seeing as the soul of that animal could have been or may become human.

Pythagoras is credited with having devised the tetractys, an important sacred symbol in later Pythagoreanism. It is the triangular figure of four rows which add up to the perfect number, ten. The Pythagoreans regarded the tetractys as a symbol of utmost mystical importance. Iamblichus, in his Life of Pythagoras, states that the tetractys was so admirable, and considered so divine by those who understood it, that Pythagoras's students would swear oaths by it.

```
        •

      •   •

    •   •   •

  •   •   •   •
```

According to Aristotle, the Pythagoreans used mathematics for solely mystical reasons, devoid of practical application. They believed that the universe and all things in it were made of numbers. Numbers were the underlying construct of everything in the universe.

Pythagoras taught that numbers vibrated, and each number produced a form. These forms produced substance. Numbers were associated with representative cosmic traits or symbology. However, at this point in the evolution of numerology related to personality traits had not been assigned to numbers.

The number one (the monad) represented the origin of all things. It was the cosmic creative force. Since odd numbers were considered male, one was the first and greatest masculine number.

The number two (the dyad) represented matter. It was the result of creation. Since even numbers were considered female, two would represent the feminine force.

The number three was an "ideal number" because it had a beginning, middle, and end. It came to represent human creativity because out of two (people – male (1) and female (2)) would come three (a child). Three was the smallest number of points that could be used to define a plane triangle, which they revered as a symbol of the god Apollo.

The number four signified the four seasons and the four elements. It is a number of limits and foundations upon which things are formed.

In the time of Pythagoras, all material was a mixture of the four elements of earth, air or wind, fire, and water. There is also a fifth element referred to as ether (aither) or spirit.

The number five represented marriage, because it was the sum of two and three. Apparently, there was a distinction between the ideas of creativity, procreation, and marriage, both in the number symbology and in Greek society at that time.

The number seven was also sacred because it was the number of planets. Only seven planets were known in the time of Pythagoras. Seven was the number of strings on a lyre, the music of which was studied by the Pythagoreans as notes, tones, vibrations, and scales. Seven was also sacred because it was associated with Apollo's birthday, which was celebrated on the seventh day of each month.

The number ten was regarded as the "perfect number." It was the conclusion, the point of returning from one to one again. It was rebirth and a new cycle. The Pythagoreans honored it by never gathering in groups larger than ten.

Pythagoras envisioned each element as a three-dimensional shape. These are referred to as the five solids. The Five Solids, also called the Platonic Solids or the Pythagorean Solids, are directly associated with particles of the elements. It is as if he put shapes to what he thought of as "atoms" or the smallest parts of earth, wind, fire, water, and ether (Aether). These particles are seen as the building blocks of reality. By using geometric figures, Pythagoras (and later Plato) connects the five solids to ideas of harmony and symmetry. The five solids are the tetrahedron, cube, octahedron, dodecahedron, and icosahedron.

Joseph Lumpkin

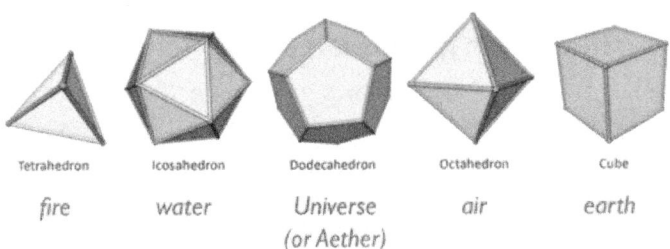

The idea of balance was so important in Pythagoras' view of the cosmos that he postulated the existence of a "Counter-Earth" situated directly opposite of us, on the other side of the sun.

All of the primary pursuits of Pythagoras and his followers were based on the principles of Numbers. These included music and astronomy/astrology and the idea that under-girting the makeup of the entire cosmos were the energies, elements, and harmonies, all of which could be qualified and quantified using the structure or expressions of numbers.
So, it was within these symbols and beliefs regarding numbers the seeds of modern Pythagorean Numerology.

How Numerology continued to develop from its simple root of basic numerical meanings to the complex system of today is shrouded in mystery. The first and most obvious possibilities go back to the Pythagorean school itself. The school was not only an occult mystery school, it was a society sworn to silence about its most closely kept secrets. There is a story regarding the cult, which reveals how zealously they guarded their secrets. It is said a student revealed the existence of the discovery of irrational numbers and for his lose tongue he was rewarded with death by drowning.

Hippassus of Metapontum, a Greek philosopher of the Pythagorean school of thought, is widely regarded as the first person to recognize the existence of irrational numbers. Supposedly, he tried to use his teacher's famous theorem $a2+b2=c2$ to find the length of the diagonal of a unit square. This revealed that a square's sides are in-commensurable with its diagonal, and this length cannot be expressed as the ratio of two integers. Since the other Pythagoreans believed that only positive rational numbers could exist, what happened next has been the subject of speculation for centuries. In short, Hippassus may have died because of his discovery. Some believe that the Pythagoreans were so horrified by the idea of in-commensurability that they threw Hippassus overboard on a sea voyage and vowed to keep the existence of irrational numbers a secret. In mathematics, the incommensurability of numbers is a ratio that cannot be expressed as a ratio of integers. It means there is no common measure between magnitudes. For example, there is no common measure between the lengths of the side and the diagonal of a square.

Irrational numbers are those which do not terminate and have no repeating pattern. Pythagoras was the first person to prove a number as an irrational number. The best example of an irrational number is 'pi' (the ratio of a circle's circumference to its diameter).

$\pi = (3.141592653589793238462643383279502884197169399375105820974.....)$

Eventually Pythagoras revealed the discovery. It is reasonable to assume other secret knowledge was kept within the school but found its way into the public in time. Part of this may well be the relationship between numbers and personality types. It is not only possible but likely Pythagoras kept the knowledge he gained in Egypt, including Chaldean numerology, to himself and delivered it with his own modifications to his students as part of his own discovery.

Letters Become Numbers

Another thing that likely contributed to the meaning of numbers was the fact they were used interchangeably with letters, and letters had meanings attached to them. In the middle east at that time, numbers were expressed by using letters. It would be like us using A to mean 1, B to mean 2, C as 3, and so forth. In the beginning of the development of alphabets each letter held a meaning, which was in turn transferred to the numbers for which they stood.

The system of numerals we use today are referred to as Arabic numerals. This is a misnomer since they were probably originally derived from India. The reason the digits are more commonly known as "Arabic numerals" in Europe and the Americas is that they were introduced to Europe in the 10th century by Arabic speakers of Spain and North Africa, who were then using the digits from Libya to Morocco.

Al-Nasawi wrote in the early 11th century that mathematicians had not agreed on the form of the numerals, but most of them had agreed to train themselves with the forms now known as Eastern Arabic numerals. The oldest written numerals are from Egypt and date to 873–874 BCE. At this time there seemed to be two types of numerals and the divergence became known as the Eastern Arabic numerals and the Western Arabic numerals. The Western Arabic numerals came to be used in the Maghreb and Al-Andalus from the 10th century onward.

Before we had separate symbols for numbers, we used letters in their place. Think of Roman Numerals, and you will get the idea. The Greeks, Romans, and Hebrews are just a few who used letters as numerals. Let us take Egyptian as an example of how letters were formed, took on meaning, and became numbers.

First, writing was based on pictographs. These were small pictures strung together to make up a story or idea. These evolved into hieroglyphs. Hieroglyphs were pictures of certain items, like a bird or a snake. The picture represented a certain sound, like our letters, but they also carried the underlying meaning of the drawing. Below is an example of how hieroglyphs looked and sounded.

Joseph Lumpkin

	A	vulture		M	owl
	B	leg		N	water
	D	hand		P	stool
	F	viper		Q	hill
	G	stand		R	mouth
	H	rope		S	cloth
	I	reed		T	loaf
	J	serpent		W	chick
	K	basket		Y	reeds
	L	lion		Z	bolt

The Hebrew letters used today were likely derived from this hieroglyphic system. The Egyptian hieroglyphs were altered and used in a Proto-Sinatic script, which in turn was altered to form the Phoenician system. It is from this Phoenician alphabet that Paleo-Hebrew was created. Slowly, the older system of letters became less like hieroglyphs and more like modern letters. The drawings were simplified into a script using more simple strokes of the stylus. These came to represent the letters of today's modern Hebrew.

There is an excellent source online that discusses how the Hebrew alphabet evolved and what meanings Paleo-Hebrew attached to various letters. – www.ancient-hebrew.org The diagram below is part of their work.

Joseph Lumpkin

Ancient Semitic/Hebrew							Modern Hebrew			Greek		Latin
Early	Middle	Late	Name	Picture	Meaning	Sound	Letter	Name	Sound	Ancient	Modern	
𐤀	† ⚹	א	El	Ox head	Strong, Power, Leader	ah, eh	א	Aleph	[silent]	A	A	A
ᗌ	᧐	ᗊ	Bet	Tent floorplan	Family, House, In	b, bh(v)	ב	Beyt	b, bh(v)	B	B	B
✓	⼁	λ	Gam	Foot	Gather, Walk	g	ג	Gimal	g	Γ	Γ	C G
▽	△	ʮ	Dal	Door	Move, Hang, Entrance	d	ד	Dalet	d	Δ	Δ	D
ᛘ	ᚩ	ᚻ	Hey	Man with arms raised	Look, Reveal, Breath	h, ah	ה	Hey	h	E	E	E
Υ	ᚩ	ᛁ	Waw	Tent peg	Add, Secure, Hook	w, o, u	ו	Vav	v	F		F
ⲋ	ⲋ	ᛁ	Zan	Mattock	Food, Cut, Nourish	z	ז	Zayin	z	Z	Z	Z
月	月	ת	Hhet	Tent wall	Wall, Outside, Divide, Half	hh	ח	Chet	hh	H	H	H
⊗	⊗	ט	Tet	Basket	Surround, Contain, Mud	t	ט	Tet	t	Θ	Θ	
ᒐ	ⳓ	ᛁ	Yad	Arm and closed hand	Hand, Work, Throw, Worship	y, ee	י	Yud	y	I	I	I J
ᛗ	ᛕ	ɔ	Kaph	Open palm	Bend, Open, Allow, Tame	k, kh	כ	Kaph	k, kh	K	K	K
ᒪ	ι	ᛁ	Lam	Shepherd Staff	Teach, Yoke, Authority, Bind	l	ל	Lamed	l	Λ	Λ	L
ᨁ	ᨁ	ᛝ	Mem	Water	Water, Chaos, Mighty, Blood	m	מ	Mem	m	M	M	M
ᛝ	ᛝ	ᛁ	Nun	Seed	Seed, Continue, Heir, Son	n	נ	Nun	n	N	N	N
ᚠ	ᚠ	ᚱ	Sin	Thorn	Grab, Hate, Protect	s	ס	Samech	s	Ξ	Ξ	X
◎	O	ᛟ	An	Eye	See, Watch, Know, Shade	[silent]	ע	Ayin	[silent]	O	O	O
ᛥ	O	ᛟ	Ghah	Rope	Twist, Dark, Wicked	gh						
ᒡ	ᒡ	ᛁ	Pey	Mouth	Open, Blow, Scatter, Edge	p, ph(f)	פ	Fey	p, ph(f)	Π	Π	P
ᚺ	ᚠ	ᚿ	Tsad	Trail	Trail, Journey, Chase, Hunt	ts	צ	Tsade	ts	M		
ᛒ	ᛩ	ᛘ	Quph	Sun on the horizon	Condense, Circle, Time	q	ק	Quph	q	Q		Q
ᛩ	ᛩ	ᛁ	Resh	Head of a man	Head, First, Top, Beginning	r	ר	Resh	r	P	P	R
ᚳ	w	ᛃ	Shin	Two front teeth	Sharp, Press, Eat, Two	sh	ש	Shin Sin	sh, s	Σ	Σ	S
+	X	ת	Taw	Crossed sticks	Mark, Sign, Signal, Monument	t	ת	Tav	t	T	T	T

Each Hebrew letter has a number associated with it. Traditionally, Hebrew numbers were written using letters, so if you look at a biblical passage in Hebrew, such as Psalms chapter 1 verse 3, it would be marked chapter א, verse ג. Most modern texts now use Arabic numerals (0,1,2,3,4, etc), however calendars and religious texts may still use the letters.

Value	Name	Letter
1	aleph	א
2	bet	ב
3	gimel	ג
4	dalet	ד
5	hay	ה
6	vav	ו
7	zayin	ז
8	khet	ח
9	tet	ט
10	yud	י
20	kaf	כ
30	lamed	ל
40	mem	מ
50	nun	נ

60	samech	ס
70	ayin	ע
80	pay	פ
90	tzadi	צ
100	kuf	ק
200	reish	ר
300	shin	ש
400	tav	ת

Note that the numbers 15 and 16 are treated specially, which if rendered as 10+5 or 10+6
would be a name of God, so they are normally written ט"ו (tet-vav, 9+6) and
ט"ז (tet zayin, 9+7).

The number associated with each letter is considered intrinsic to the meaning of that letter. For example, א indicates the Creator, as God is the One source of everything. We have already established that the Romans used letters as numerals. These were once taught in school and every child knew his or her Roman Numerals. Greeks used the same system of substitution. Below is an example. The designations of ARL,

The Enneagram: Its Source, History, Development, and Meaning

TNR refer to different fonts used to render the Hebrew or Greek letters. Arial font, Times New Roman... NV is numerical value. OV is ordinal value. P is pronunciation.

	THE BIBLE - ALPHABETS AND NUMERICAL VALUES													
	Hebrew					Syr	Greek					
OV	ARL	TNR	NV	P	Name			ARL	TNR	NV	P	Name
1	א	א	1	(a)	Alef	ܐ	A	A	α	A	α	1	A	Alpha
2	ב	ב	2	B,V	Bet	ܒ	B	B	β	B	β	2	B,V	Beta
3	ג	ג	3	G	Gimel	ܓ	Γ	Γ	γ	Γ	γ	3	G	Gamma
4	ד	ד	4	D	Dalet	ܕ	Δ	Δ	δ	Δ	δ	4	D	Delta
5	ה	ה	5	H	He	ܗ	E	E	ε	E	ε	5	E	Epsilon
6	ו	ו	6	W,V	Vav	ܘ		F,Ϛ	F,ϛ	F,C	F,ϛ	6	W	Digamma*
7	ז	ז	7	Z	Zayin	ܙ	Z	Z	ζ	Z	ζ	7	Z	Zeta
8	ח	ח	8	H,X	Chet	ܚ	H	H	η	H	η	8	E	Eta
9	ט	ט	9	T	Tet	ܛ	Θ	Θ	θ	Θ	θ	9	Th	Theta
10	י	י	10	J,I,Y	Yod	ܝ	I	I	ι	I	ι	10	I,J	Iota
11	כך	כך	20	K,X	Kaph	ܟ	K	K	κ	K	κ	20	K,C	Kappa
12	ל	ל	30	L	Lamed	ܠ	Λ	Λ	λ	Λ	λ	30	L	Lambda
13	מם	מם	40	M	Mem	ܡ	M	M	μ	M	μ	40	M	Mu
14	נן	נן	50	N	Nun	ܢ	N	N	ν	N	ν	50	N	Nu
15	ס	ס	60	S	Samekh	ܣ	Ξ	Ξ	ξ	Ξ	ξ	60	Ks	Xi
16	ע	ע	70	(o)	Ayin	ܥ	O	O	ο	O	ο	70	O	Omicron
17	פף	פף	80	P,F	Pe	ܦ	Π	Π	π	Π	π	80	P	Pi
18	צץ	צץ	90	Ts	Tsade	ܨ		Ϙ,Ϟ	Ϙ,ϟ	Ϙ,Ϟ	Ϙ,ϟ	90	K,Q	Qoppa
19	ק	ק	100	K,Q	Qoph	ܩ	P	P	ρ	P	ρ	100	R	Rho
20	ר	ר	200	R	Resh	ܪ	C	Σ	σ,ς	Σ	σ,ς	200	S	Sigma
21	ש	ש	300	S,Sh	Shin	ܫ	T	T	τ	T	τ	300	T	Tau
22	ת	ת	400	T	Tav	ܬ	Y	Y	υ	Y	υ	400	U,Y	Upsilon
23							Φ	Φ	φ	Φ	φ	500	Ph	Phi
24							X	X	χ	X	χ	600	Kh	Chi
25							Ψ	Ψ	ψ	Ψ	ψ	700	Ps	Psi
26							Ω	Ω	ω	Ω	ω	800	O	Omega
27								Ϡ,Ϟ	Ϡ,ϟ	Ϡ,Ϟ	Ϡ,ϟ	900	Ts	Sampi

It is difficult to know how the meaning of numbers according to modern numerology came to be. It is reasonable to speculate that Pythagoras placed his mystical meanings on each number. In time, his students expanded the meanings based on the symbology building within their mystery school and the society using the alphabet, and thus, the numbering system being used. It is likely the meanings in other ancient spiritual texts were used to augment their knowledge of the meanings of each number.

The Chaldean Approach

Assuming Pythagoras came in contact with Chaldean numerology before teaching his own ideas about numbers, it seems right to start with a brief overview of Chaldean numerology.

Chaldia was a region located in the mountainous interior of the eastern Black Sea, around northeast Turkey. During the reign of the Byzantine emperor Justinian I (c. 527–565) the tribes in the area were subdued, conquered, and Christianized. Justinian included the entire region in the newly constituted province. During the Late Middle Ages, it was a stronghold of the Empire of Trebizond until its fall to the Ottoman Empire in 1461.

According to the Chaldean system, all the alphabets are assigned a number from 1 to 8.

The number 9 was left out by the ancient people because it was considered to be a holy number. Nine does have a meaning, since it does appear often as an end result, but there is no letter assigned to the number nine.

Chaldean numerology was introduced for the first time in Mesopotamia and Western Astrology is also said to have been invented in Mesopotamia. Many numerologists have tried to connect Chaldean numerology and astrology. This type of numerology systems is very closely related to the Vedic system that is present in India. The Chaldean system states that every individual letter has its own inherent vibration which is determined by its state of energy. According to this state, a number from 1 to 8 is assigned to the respective letters. There is also a number 9 which is not mixed or displayed with the other numbers. The number 9 is considered together with the other numbers only when it is the total sum result of the rest of the numbers. All of this is done because according to the legends of Chaldean numerology, the number 9 has a significant value and is also the most sacred number. The chart equating letters to numbers may lack the number 9, but when the numbers are added, a 9 can occur. According to studies, when single numbers are displayed in this form of numerology, it is used to depict the outer qualities or personality of the person.

On the basis of Chaldean, the numbers linked to the letters in the name are as follows:

1	2	3	4	5	6	7	8
A	B	C	D	E	U	O	F
I	K	G	M	H	V	Z	P
J	R	L	T	N	W		
Q		S		X			
Y							

The above chart is applied to the full name of the person in the following manner:

John Jay Smith

1755 111 34145 All numbers for each name are added together.

18   3   17   Those numbers are added, equaling 38. Then the digits are added until a single digit remains.

3+8=11 1+1 =2 The number 2 represents the entire name and the basic personality of the individual.

There are also certain applications for the vowels and consonants.

In numerology, the vowels are said to reveal the heart's desire. This is what you want out of life and yourself on a deep level.

The consonants represent your outward personality. It is how you express yourself. It is the mask shown to the outside world.

The entire name, with all letters included, is the personality number. It is also referred to as the destiny number. This number represents the fullness of the person as it combines what we desire to be and how we express ourselves. These things make up our personality. This number, which is derived from the full name, is the only number we will focus on in this book since this is not meant to be a book on numerology. If you wish to dive deeper into numerology, I suggest "Numerology, A Book of Insights", by Anne Burton, published in 2006 by Fifth Estate Publishing.

The vowels of John Jay Smith are O,A,Y, and I. The Y is considered a vowel in English when it makes the vowel in front of it long or when it has an "E" sound. It is a consonant when it has sound of its own, such as Yard or Yawn. The O,A,Y,I are 7,1,1,1 and equal 10, which reduces to 1.
The consonants of John Jay Smith are added and reduced as follows:

$$1\ 55\ 1\quad 34\quad 45\ =\ 28\quad 2+8 = 10\quad 1+0 = 1$$

Basic meanings for each number in the Chaldean systems are explained below. Here, we begin to see the extraordinary similarity to the meanings within the Enneagram. You will note the meanings for types 7 and 5 are reversed. The type description for a 7 in numerology will be very similar to the meaning of the Enneagram type 5, and a numerology 5 will align with the Enneagram type 7. The meaning and sequence of types in numerology may make a difference since calculations are used, but they make little to no difference in the Enneagram system since the numbers are used mostly as a "handle" or name. We could use any name for the nine types in the Enneagram and, as long as the terms were understood, it would make no difference.

Below are the nine personalities, according to Chaldean numerology:

Numerology number 1
Ones have a strong will and a winner's mentality. Ones dislike authorities because they want to be the authority. Because they wish to lead, they like to delegate work. It makes them feel important. Ones are critical, judging others by a high standard. They will not tolerate jobs or results that are less than perfect, and they will not tolerate people without ambition. Ones are perfectionists. They are creative leaders

who can think outside the norms. Ones do not like complex problems because they think success should come easily to them. They want success and the freedom it brings, even at the expense of others.

Numerology number 2

Twos are soft and often weak willed. They are emphatic and can use this gift to be manipulative. Twos can easily become sad and melancholic. However, from their sadness can flow creativity. The main strength of the Two is that they are good at reading and understanding people. They have strong empathy, but this can be used as a tool to ward passive-aggressive manipulation. Twos are detail oriented, but they can become bogged down in detail and fail to see the big picture. It is the nature of humans to over-compensate, therefore some who are Twos, even though they feel weak, may become criminals and tough guys in order to appear strong even though they are afraid.

Numerology number 3

The number Three is part of the sacred Triad of 3, 6 and 9. Three represent expansion, growth, birth, and creation. Threes have a quick mind, so it is the number of theories, knowledge, and advancement.

They have a talent for being strategic and keeping an overview. Threes are unique and so they want to do everything themselves in order to put their personal style and flair to it. They are concerned with personal image and presentation. Although Threes are not as critical as the number One, they still want to be in control to be sure that everything is done and presented well and that the project is marked with their special panache.

Numerology number 4

People who are represented by the number Four want to be unique. They are afraid of going unnoticed or unrecognized. They are natural-born engineers, scientists, and inventors of all kinds.

Fours want to revolutionize the world with new ideas and concepts. Many times, they lack the tenacity, funds, or self-discipline to bring their new ideas to life, so they feel stuck, forgotten, rejected, and resentful. Generally, people hate new ideas that challenge their comfort zone, so there is always resistance to overcome.

People who are represented by the number 4 are often perceived as the black sheep.

Many times, they suffer psychological problems, drug abuse, alcoholism, or melancholia.

Numerology number 5

Fives are natural born communicators. They have the ability to work a room, make friends, and network. Their social skills are high, and they are good at reading people. Fives get along with everyone, except those who they deem to be controlling. No one should come between a Five and their freedom. In Chaldean numerology, Five is thought to be the "swing" or "pivot" number because it is between 1 and 9. Thus it is quixotic. A social butterfly.

Five represents motion, vigor, communication, friends, and activity. The energy can be directed socially, sexually, or via business.

Numerology number 6

Six is the second number of the sacred Triad of 3, 6 and 9. In some ways, Sixes tend to be the opposite of Three. Three is about doing and presenting and the number 6 is about receiving.
Therefore, the number 6 stands for comfort, the home-body, the conservative. Sixes are slow movers and they are very stubborn.
The Six comes across as charming, trustworthy, and loyal, however, if they become angry or feel like they have been unfairly treated, they will seek revenge. Sixes can be

Machiavellian, using manipulation and charm for personal gain.

Numerology number 7

Sevens are the introverts, philosophers, academics, mystics, and sagas among us. Sevens seek the deeper meaning in life but can get lost down the rabbit hole. They live within their minds and at times become trapped there. Sevens have a natural understanding of human psychology because they are the observers of people and life. But because they tend to observe instead of participate, they can become lonely and detached. Even through the detachment, or maybe because of it, Sevens tend to be intuitive. Sevens will overcompensate at times, becoming reckless, and even violent.

Numerology number 8

In Chaldean numerology, the number Eight is a powerful number. Eights are driven, willful, intelligent people who are born to change, or at least challenge, the world.

People who are represented by the number 8 want to build things up slowly and thoroughly.

They challenge the status quo, the accepted authorities, and traditional order. Eights can be cynical and pushy. They are practical in their approach to life and jobs. Many Eights had a difficult childhood, where they had to overcome challenges or fight to survive. This made them distrust authority figures, who let them down and did not protect them. This made them tough enough to deal with major obstacles and responsibilities. Eight is the number of the business owner, the boss, the CEO, and those in high levels of authority.

Numerology number 9
Nine is the terminus of the sacred Triad of 3, 6 and 9. It is three threes and is the highest of the numbers. It is the conclusion of the matter. Whereas zero is nothing, Nine is everything. According to ancient Chaldean philosophy, these states are the same. This is Karma coming full circle. Therefore, Nines are focused on the highest forms of altruistic love, divine justice, honor, and integrity. Nines speak their mind openly and clearly. They speak out against injustice and wrong doing. Like Eights, Nines had a tough childhood with many coming from broken homes or homes with neglectful or abusive parents. This engenders compassion and the ability to see things from many angles. However, by seeing all sides, Nines can have trouble making decisions or motivating themselves to break from the status quo. They may feel stuck, like being pulled from all sides.

Vedic Numerology

The accepted hypothesis is that Chaldean numerology branched off from Vedic numerology.
Chaldean numerology is considered by many to be the original system, but in reality, the Vedic numerology system from India is the original system of numerology and the Chaldean system is a branch of the Vedic system. Pythagorean numerology is a later comer, arriving after Alexander conquered Babylonia and the Greek's had access to Chaldean wisdom and scriptures. Let's look deeper into the concepts of Vedic or Indian Numerology.

Vedic numerology has roots in the ancient Indian Vedas. A text titled Anka Shastra addresses this discipline. One of the modern downfalls of numerology is that of changing languages and alphabets. It seems somewhat arbitrary. If one calculates, for example, the name Theo in English we get one number, and then if we calculate it in Greek the Th is replaced with the letter Theta, E with Eta, and O with Omicron to yield a totally different personality number, due to the change of writing systems or alphabets. Vedic numerology does away with alphabets. It uses vibratory resonance of the syllables in the name and associates a sound with a number.

The sound vibrations produced by the sounds of one's name have a relation with the vibrations of the numbers.

The following is a small example of the conversion of certain phonemes and their relationship to numerical vibrations, given in the Sankhya Sastra by Kapila Rishi:

Ka 1   Cha 6   t'Ta 1   Tha 6   Pa 1

Kha 2 Chha 7 t'Tha 2 Thha 7 Pha 2

Ga 3   Ja 8   d'Da 3   Dha 8   Ba 3

Gha 4 Jha 9   d'Dha 4 Dhha 9 Bha 4

n'Ga 5 n'Ja 5 n'Na 5   Na 5   Ma 5

Ya 1   Ra 2   La 3   Va 4

Ha 8   Y'sh 7 Sha 6   Sa 5

Other sources expand the chart as follows:

1 2 3 4 5 6 7 8 9 0

Ka group

ka kha ga gha na ca cha ja jha na(nasel)

Ta group

ta tha da dha ng ta tha da dha n (as in nyet)

Fa group

pa pha ba bha ma

Ya group

ya ra la va sa sha ha ksa jna

All vowel sounds or A,E,I,O,U, long and short, are = 0

Some charts also count a rolled R (as in Spanish) and Rh as 0.

Later in history, when the Latin Alphabet came into use and was bolstered by the take over of India by England, numbers were attached to the alphabet.

1-A,I,J,Q,Y

2-B,K,R   3-C,G,L,S

4-D,M,T 5-E,H,N,X

6-U,V,W 7-O,Z

8-F,P

The mystical Indian culture sees numbers as symbols, and those symbols are like drawings. They convey a meaning due to their shape. This takes us full circle from our discussion on how letters themselves were formed from pictures and hieroglyphs.

0	zero	०	शून्य	Shuniye
1	one	१	एक	Ek
2	two	२	दो	Do
3	three	३	तीन	Teen
4	four	४	चार	Char
5	five	५	पांच	Panch
6	six	६	छह	Cheh
7	seven	७	सात	Saat
8	eight	८	आठ	Aath
9	nine	९	नौ	Nao
10	ten	१०	दस	Das
11	eleven	११	ग्यारह	Gyaarah
12	twelve	१२	बारह	Baarah
13	thirteen	१३	तेरह	Tehrah
14	fourteen	१४	चौदह	Chaudah
15	fifteen	१५	पंद्रह	Pandrah

One

The emanation of the awakened Brahman which created all that is. The mind cannot grasp him. He is the creator of gods. Brahma, Vishnu, and Shiva were from him. He is beyond the mind's grasp, but to experience him is to know bliss. One is Atman – the individual self. But in the end, Atman and Brahman are the same. In the Advaita Vedanta (non-dualism) philosophy, the Atman, which is the individual soul or self within each living entity is fully identical to Brahman. The Advaita school believes that there is a single soul that exists in all living beings. The Atman is an illusion, or more accurately, an individual perception of Brahman. There is no Atman (self) separate from Brahman (god). There is a single reality and oneness that unifies all beings. All are equally divine. One is "I alone am everything." There is no duality.

Two

Two represents a state of duality. It is the illusion brought about by our minds and the senses through objective experience, in which ego boundaries are erected between the observer and the observed. Two symbolizes the false gulf or split between Brahman and Atman. The knower and the known are the same. The creator and the creation. The subject and the object are one. Two is the one God creator and the Prakriti or nature, which is the creation.

Each individual is the peak of a wave in the same ocean. The wave and ocean are not separate. Two is this illusion of difference. The concept of Two (Me and the Other) is the cause of our suffering. To resolve the problem, we must attain the One and realize we are all one and we are one with God. This will allow us to reach Zero, which is nirvana.

Three

God created all. Brahman manifested everything, but Rtam is the rhythm of the universal that imposes order. It is the vibrations, frequencies, and cycles guiding the entire creation, just as the gears within a clock for the whole of creation. This is the dance of Siva. It is the seasons, times, cycles, frequencies, processions, and events tying nature together. God is truly orderly.

Three is the balance between Brahma, Vishnu, and Siva- the creator, the preserver, and the destroyer. The interaction of these three is the pattern of all things. It is Vishnu, the preserver, that guards the Rtam and keeps the universe in play by protecting the rhythmic cycles of the cosmic clock.

That which deviates too far from its rhythm or course wonders beyond his protection and is destroyed by Siva. Three is the number of the sacred vocative, AUM. The sound of consciousness. The power that makes body and mind animate and aware.

Four

Four is the number of ego and the awareness of self. The detachment from creation forms a false self, which gives way to desires. This is Maya, the illusion that drives us deep into darkness and delusion. The only way out is to follow the path of righteousness, in order to set things right again. This path is called Dharma.

Dharma is a system of religious and moral laws given to us to navigate our journey toward freedom or salvation. The aim of dharma preserves the divine order. All of creation is divine, and all the cosmos was created to uphold dharma. The divine order. Many gods seen in Hindu iconography have four arms because they enforce dharma, and the number four represents Dharma.

Five

Five represents the physical universe, the physical body, and the earth. There are five elements, and the earth is the fifth element.

The elements are Ether (akasa), which is the essence of spirit and thus God. It is omnipresent. It was and is eternal. Air (Vayu), which is as close to ether as we can get on this earthly plane. Unlike ether, we can sense air. Fire (Agni) is the third element. It takes air to make fire and unlike air, fire has form, color, and heat. Water (Jalam) is the fourth element. It gives life and can take it. Life rides upon it and in it. Water feeds the earth. Earth is the fifth element. It is the densest of all elements but because of its structure, life springs from it. As we have looked at the elements, we can see they have gotten denser and denser with each element. Here with number five, we see the fullness of the physical body and its five senses of sight, sound, smell, touch, and taste. Five is the number of change. When a person dies, they take on the fifth state because their breath, heat, water, and body have been left behind.

Six

Six represents the highest and lowest state the human mind can reach. There are five outer senses, but some say awareness or intuition, coming from the mind, makes up the sixth sense. The mind guides us toward the highest and lowest states of knowledge and ignorance, which leads to bondage and liberation. The Upanishads declare:

> All that we are is the result of what we have thought: it is founded on our thoughts; it is made up of our thoughts.
> If a man speaks or acts with an evil thought, pain follows him, as the wheel follows the foot of the ox that draws the carriage.
> All that we are is the result of what we have thought: it is founded on our thoughts; it is made up of our thoughts.
> If a man speaks or acts with a pure thought, happiness follows him, like a shadow that never leaves him.
> (Müller)

All mind is covered over, unobstructed with the senses, but in a pure, undisturbed mind shines the radiance of Atman.

It is said, the holy man has six duties: teaching, studying, performing sacrifice (the ritual), offering sacrifice (the inward heart of giving), and charity (alms).

Seven

Seven represents the earthly plane. But it is also the number of spiritual practice. Hindu scriptures declare there are seven planes above the earth and seven below. The physical earth is the middle plane.

There are seven chakras.

1. The Root Chakra - Muladhara (Red)
2. The Sacral Chakra - Svadhisthana (Orange)
3. The Solar Plexus Chakra - Manipura (Yellow)
4. The Heart Chakra - Anahata (Green)
5. The Throat Chakra - Vishuddha (Sky Blue)
6. The Third Eye Chakra - Ajna (Indigo)
7. The Crown Chakra - Sahasrara (Violet/White)

Seven Hindu sages, known as saptarishis, channeled the Vedas and other texts from the higher planes into our earthly plane. The sages were said to have been born from the very mind of Brahma, who descended from Ursa Major to teach the Vedas.

There are seven musical notes corresponding to the seven planes of consciousness. Hindu scriptures are replete with the number seven. There are seven tongues, seven flames, seven spheres, and seven energies that awaken during spiritual practice.

Eight

Eight is the number of wealth and power.

The consort of Vishnu was the goddess Lakshmi. She has eight forms. They are:

Adi Lakshmi (the first and complete form), Dhanya Lakshmi (wealth of agriculture), Dhairya Lakshmi (wealth of courage), Gaja Lakshmi (wealth of livestock), Santana Lakshmi (wealth of offspring), Vijaya Lakshmi (wealth of business), Vidya Lakshmi (wealth of knowledge), and Dhana Lakshmi (wealth of money).

Shaktis are the female energies, abilities, or powers, from the primordial cosmic energy that are thought to pervade the universe. Shakti is thought of as a creative, sustaining force, and an equal and opposite balancing destructive force. There are eight Shakti of Lord Vishnu: Sridevi (goddess of money), Bhudevi (goddess of land), Sarasvathi (goddess of knowledge), Priti (goddess of happiness), Kirti (goddess of fame), Santi (goddess of peace), Tusti (goddess of pleasure) and Pusti (goddess of health). Corresponding with them again are the eight consorts of Lord Krishna.

There are eight lords of direction over the eight sections of North, South, East, West, North-East, South-East, North-West and South-West.

Nine

Nine is the number of completion. Nine represents the completion of form, function, and journey.

There are nine forms of worship: hearing about God, singing about God, mindfulness of God, serving in the temple, worshiping God, praying to God, Doing service in Holy causes (serving in missions), communing with God, and surrendering to God.

In Hindu astronomy, we recognize nine planets: the Sun, the Moon, Mars, Mercury, Jupiter, Venus, Saturn, Rahu, and Ketu. Astronomically, Rahu and Ketu denote the points of intersection of the paths of the Sun and the Moon. They are the north and the south lunar nodes.

Our body is the city of nine gates in which Atman resides. The nine gates refer to the nine openings of our two eyes, two ears, two nostrils, navel, anus, and urethra. We are called a temple with nine gates.

Pythagorean Numerology

We have already discussed the history of Pythagoras and the fact that he may have been exposed to mystical teachings regarding numbers when he visited Egypt and the surrounding areas. We have seen how Chaldean numerology uses one through eight to break down the letters in the name into numbers. We have explored Vedic numerology, which is thought to have given rise to the Chaldean system. Now we will take a look at the system that was informed from Chaldean numerology, which is known as Pythagorean Numerology.

As we look at the chart showing the relationship between letters and numbers, we see Pythagoras uses all numbers from one to nine and the relationship between letters and numbers differ from Chaldean numerology.

1	2	3	4	5	6	7	8	9
a	b	c	d	e	f	j	h	i
j	k	l	m	n	o	p	q	r
s	t	u	v	w	x	y	z	

The same calculation is used as in Chaldean numerology to find the personality number, but this time we use the relationship of letters to numbers shown above.

John Jay Smith

1685 117 14928

  20 + 9 + 24 =53   5+3 = 8

In this system of numerology, this gent is an 8 personality number.

There are also slight differences in the meaning of the numbers.

Below we have the basic meaning for each number in the Pythagorean numerology system.

Later we will do a side by side comparison of the full meaning of each number in the systems of numerology and enneagram.

TYPE ONE

Positive ones are self-assured natural leaders, reliable, productive, motivated, self starters, and they are idealists.

  Negative ones are judgmental, inflexible, self-righteous, critical, controlling, and perfectionists. They can't stand to be wrong.

  Fault line - reactive, angry, over reaction to a critical internal voice leads to defensive anger. In their fight not to be wrong they turn to a false self righteousness.

TYPE TWO

Positive twos are loving, helping, caring, sensitive, and supportive. They have good attention to detail. They are the diplomats.

Negative twos are passive/aggressive, manipulative, emotionally weak, given to feelings of martyrdom. They have the egotism that comes from thinking that they are secretly behind the scenes making things happen. They have the idea that people could not get along without them.

Fault line - emotion repression. Unsure of their own feelings. Taking on the feelings of others. Trying to control though passive/aggressive manipulation. They can become hostile if they don't think that they are properly appreciated, even though they have manipulated to get things done.

TYPE THREE

Positive threes are optimistic, confident, energetic, outgoing, social, good networkers and communicators.

Negative threes are vain, deceptive, shallow, vindictive, jealous, competitive, and perfectionists. They play the part that they have chosen to the hilt.

Fault line - deceit of self and others. An identity crisis occurs when their likes, dislikes, and feelings are suspended in order to portray what they decide is appropriate...the need to fit into the character that they have chosen means that at times they lose themselves in their part.

TYPE FOUR

Positive fours are warm, physical, creative, logical, and down to earth, with a realistic approach to life.
Negative fours are depressed, guilt driven, stubborn, moody, self-absorbed, and obsessed with what they think they could have been.

Fault line - a feeling of being wronged or held down. Self pity. A dramatic or uncentered way of expressing feelings such as addictions.

TYPE FIVE

Positive fives are fun loving, spontaneous, imaginative, productive, quick, confident, curious, and charming.

Negative fives are narcissistic, impulsive, undisciplined, restless, rebellious, unfocused, critical, and curt. They are masters at rationalization.

Fault line - a pervading feeling of emptiness is the force which drives the five to try and find an experience, or something in the physical world to fill the void. Greed and gluttony is the fault line.

TYPE SIX

Positive sixes are loyal, caring, practical, parental, responsible, and care-givers.

Negative sixes are judgmental, rigid, defensive, unpredictable, and paranoid. They distrust authority but need approval. This sets up a love\hate relationship.

Fault line - the fear of not being approved, together with the fear of authority figures, can get strong enough to tint the six's entire outlook. This is paranoia.

TYPE SEVEN

Positive sevens are objective, wise, self-contained observers.

Negative sevens are snobbish, arrogant, stingy, critical, aloof, and emotionally removed.

Fault line - an attempt to fill the emptiness within is done with knowledge. As long as they are involved with the mind, it takes their attention off of what they are feeling, (and what they are not feeling). They believe completely in the old adage that knowledge is power, especially when it is a secret to control someone with.

TYPE EIGHT

Positive eights are direct, authoritative, driven, self-confident, capable, and assertive people with a strong sense of self.

Negative eights are controlling, insensitive, self-centered, domineering, aggressive, intimidating, and bullies.

Fault line - a lust for power and control of their environment spreads out to include the people in it. There is an anger at not having everything in control and operating correctly or according to their wishes.

TYPE NINE

The positive nine is pleasant, peaceful, generous, receptive, and open minded.

The negative nine is apathetic and forgetful. They vacillate between unassertive and stubborn; obsessive and apathetic.

Fault line - nines have the tendency to "zone-out or space-out". They think that if they do nothing then what is bothering them may go away. They can become passive/aggressive as they try to ignore their anger and disappointment. They fear change and want to keep things as they are. A known condition is preferable even if it is bad.

Pythagorean – It is said that in the 6th century BC he could even predict the occurrence of certain events just by using certain numbers. Based on the position of Greek alphabets in the entire sequence, the numbers were assigned accordingly.

Over the centuries, the various types of numerology borrowed from each other, mixing and cross-pollinating to form the systems we have today.

Bible Number Symbology

In our timeline we have traced the ancient wisdom from India to Chaldea, into the Middle East, and now finally to Greece, where it spread from there. This may have been the route by which Gurdjieff encountered the ancient knowledge since Gurdjieff's father was a Caucasus Greek, Yiannis Georgiades. Gurdjieff could have encountered older versions of the wisdom, such as the Chaldean system while in Iran, or even the original system, while he was visiting India. According to his own account, Gurdjieff's traveled to Central Asia, Egypt, Iran, India, Tibet, and Rome. This route made up the major areas responsible for the growth and evolution of numerology taught today. But, before we end our journey tracing the path of numerology, let us complete our study with Pythagorean numerology in Greece.

We are told one of the sources Gurdjieff and his student pulled from to form theories on personality and personal growth was the Holy Bible. The hidden meaning in the scriptures he called esoteric Christianity. Within the Bible there is number symbology.

The Number 1 symbolizes unity and absolute singleness. Monad, monotheism, one god.

The Number 2 represents the duality that is consistent with both flesh and spirit. It is the number of the witness. It is the comparison and contrast between two things. The balanced arbitrator. A friend. A helper. A mate.

The Number 3 is the first sacred number after one. It is divine completeness. Number 3 represents the trinity in the New Testament.

The Number 4 represents a foundation of work. There are four corners of the earth, four kingdoms mentioned in Daniel's prophecy, four seasons and four primary directions (east, west, north, and south). This means it is the number of limits being set.

The Number 5 symbolizes God's grace and kindness upon humankind. There are 10 commandments divided into 2 parts. There are 5 external laws governing our actions and 5 internal laws guarding the heart and attitude. Pentateuch are the 5 books of Moses containing God's law and there are five divisions of Psalms.

The Number 6 is related to the limitations and shortcomings of mankind. It represents our failure, sins, and human weakness.

On the sixth day, mankind was created by God. The number 666 represents completeness but for sin and evil. It is a number related to Satan.

The Number 7 is considered to be one of the holiest numbers in Christianity. In Scripture, seven often symbolizes completion or perfection. Genesis tells us that God created the heavens and the Earth in six days, and, upon completion, God rested on the seventh day (Genesis 1; 2:1-2).

The Number 8 represents hopes for a bright future and a new beginning. This is so because God spoke 8 words to start creating and Jesus chose the 8th day after his death to resurrect. St. Augustine gave us a brief explanation of the significance of the 8th day in his dispute with Faustus. Augustine wrote, "Christ suffered voluntarily, and so could choose His own time for suffering and for resurrection, He brought it about that His body rested from all its works on Sabbath in the tomb, and that His resurrection on the third day, which we call the Lord's day, the day after the Sabbath, and therefore the eighth, proved the circumcision of the eighth day to be also prophetical of Him. For what does circumcision mean, but the eradication of the mortality which comes from our carnal generation?"

The Number 9 is conclusion. In the Bible, the number nine, being three times three, represents a full cycle, finality, and divine completeness. In order to save humanity, Jesus died at 3 pm, which is the 9th hour. The Jews and Romans divided the day in terms of military watch shifts, each being roughly three hours long. Sunup was considered to be around 6AM, meaning 3PM would have been considered the 9th hour of the day. Number nine is also related to qualities like gentleness, kindness, love, peace, belief, loyalty, happiness, suffering and self-moderation.

The Numbers of the Tribes of Israel

On the surface the bible does not have much to say about personalities, that is until we dig deeper and look closely at the attitudes and actions of central figures. The Old Testament is written about and for the Jewish people. These people were broken into twelve tribes. Each tribe began with a man who had certain traits, which became part of the general makeup of the tribe. Let us look at each of these leaders.

A View of the Sons – the Tribes – the Personalities

As was the custom in the days of Jacob, his sons were born of several different women. Both wives and handmaidens were mothers to the twelve sons of Jacob. Some sons made a direct and immediate impact on the world. Others raised sons and daughters who, in turn, grew into tribes which produced men and women of historical impact. The deeds, actions, and personalities of these men, along with the insights and blessings of Jacob given to each son at the time of Jacob's death announce the kind of men they were and the traits of the tribes the sons would produce.

In the end, ten of the twelve tribes would disappear, leaving only two tribes still able to trace their roots back to the beginning.

In 930 BC, ten tribes formed the independent Kingdom of Israel in the north and the two other tribes, Judah and Benjamin, set up the southern Kingdom of Judah. Following in 721 BCE the Assyrians over ran the ten northern tribes. After their defeat, the ten tribes gradually assimilated into the surrounding societies and vanished from history.

Let us look at their legacies of personality.

Reuben, The First Son

Reuben, the first son, was a leader. He was headstrong, selfish, and rash. Although his rashness and selfishness made him unstable, he was considered a force of strength and might. Many times he would act on impulse, only to regret his actions. Because he was a leader, others suffered from his decisions

GEN 29:32 And Leah conceived, and bare a son, and she called his name Reuben: for she said, Surely the LORD hath looked upon my affliction; now therefore my husband will love me.

GEN 35:22 And it came to pass, when Israel dwelt in that land, that Reuben went and lay with Bilhah his father's concubine: and Israel heard it. Now the sons of Jacob were twelve:

GEN 49:2 Gather yourselves together, and hear, ye sons of Jacob; and hearken unto Israel your father. Reuben, thou art my firstborn, my might, and the beginning of my strength, the excellency of dignity, and the excellency of power: Unstable as water, thou shalt not excel; because thou wentest up to thy father's bed; then defilest thou it: he went up to my couch.

GEN 37:17 And the man said, they are departed hence; for I heard them say, Let us go to Dothan. And Joseph went after his brethren, and found them in Dothan. 18 And when they saw him afar off, even before he came near unto them, they conspired against him to slay him. 19 And they said one to another, Behold, this dreamer cometh. 20 Come now therefore, and let us slay him, and cast him into some pit, and we will say, some evil beast hath devoured him: and we shall see what will become of his dreams. 21 And Reuben heard it, and he delivered him out of their hands; and said, let us not kill him. 22 And Reuben said unto them, shed no blood, but cast him into this pit that is in the wilderness, and lay no hand upon him; that he might rid him out of their hands, to deliver him to his father again.

GEN 37:28 Then there passed by Midianites merchantmen; and they drew and lifted up Joseph out of the pit, and sold Joseph to the Ishmaelites for twenty pieces of silver: and they brought Joseph into Egypt. 29And Reuben returned unto the pit; and, behold, Joseph was not in the pit; and he rent his clothes. 30 And he returned unto his brethren, and said, the child is not; and I, whither shall I go?

Simeon, The Second Son

Simeon was a politician. He was a diplomat with an agenda. He was able to persuade others he had their best interest at heart, all the while planning their downfall. He did not fight head to head but would set up emotional and political scenarios to manipulate and entrap others. He used subterfuge to get his way. This personality type must choose between diplomacy and duplicity.

GEN 29:33 And she conceived again, and bare a son; and said, Because the LORD hath heard I was hated, he hath therefore given me this son also: and she called his name Simeon.

GEN 34:1 And Dinah the daughter of Leah, which she bares unto Jacob, went out to see the daughters of the land. 2 And when Shechem the son of Hamor the Hivite, prince of the country, saw her, he took her, and lay with her, and defiled her. 3 And his soul clave unto Dinah the daughter of Jacob, and he loved the damsel, and spake kindly unto the damsel. 4 And Shechem spake unto his father Hamor, saying, Get me this damsel to wife. 5 And Jacob heard that he had defiled Dinah his daughter: now his sons were with his cattle in the field: and Jacob held his peace until they were come. 6 And Hamor the father of Shechem went out unto Jacob to commune with him.7 And the sons of Jacob came out of the field when they heard it: and the men were grieved, and they were very wroth, because he had wrought folly in Israel in lying with Jacob's daughter: which thing ought not to be done.

GEN 34:8 And Hamor communed with them, saying, the soul of my son Shechem longeth for your daughter: I pray you give her him to wife. 9 And make ye marriages with us, and give your daughters unto us, and take our daughters unto you. 10 And ye shall dwell with us: and the land shall be before you; dwell and trade ye therein, and get you possessions therein. 11 And Shechem said unto her father and unto her brethren, let me find grace in your eyes, and what ye shall say unto me I will give. 12 Ask me never so much dowry and gift, and I will give according as ye shall say unto me: but give me the damsel to wife. 13 And the sons of Jacob answered Shechem and Hamor his father deceitfully, and said, because he had defiled Dinah their sister:

14 And they said unto them, we cannot do this thing, to give our sister to one that is uncircumcised; for that were a reproach unto us: 15 But in this will we consent unto you: If ye will be as we be, that every male of you be circumcised; 16 Then will we give our daughters unto you, and we will take your daughters to us, and we will dwell with you, and we will become one people. 17 But if ye will not hearken unto us, to be circumcised; then will we take our daughter, and we will be gone. 18 And their words pleased Hamor, and Shechem Hamor's son. 19 And the young man deferred not to do the thing, because he had delight in Jacob's daughter: and he was more honorable than all the house of his father.

20 And Hamor and Shechem his son came unto the gate of their city, and communed with the men of their city, saying, 21 These men are peaceable with us; therefore let them dwell in the land, and trade therein; for the land, behold, it is large enough for them; let us take their daughters to us for wives, and let us give them our daughters. 22 Only herein will the men consent unto us for to dwell with us, to be one people, if every male among us be circumcised, as they are circumcised. 23 Shall not their cattle and their substance and every beast of

theirs be ours? Only let us consent unto them, and they will dwell with us.

GEN 34:24 And unto Hamor and unto Shechem his son hearkened all that went out of the gate of his city; and every male was circumcised, all that went out of the gate of his city. 25 And it came to pass on the third day, when they were sore, that two of the sons of Jacob, Simeon and Levi, Dinah's brethren, took each man his sword, and came upon the city boldly, and slew all the males. 26 And they slew Hamor and Shechem his son with the edge of the sword, and took Dinah out of Shechem's house, and went out. 27 The sons of Jacob came upon the slain, and spoiled the city, because they had defiled their sister. 28 They took their sheep, and their oxen, and their asses, and that which was in the city, and that which was in the field, 29 And all their wealth, and all their little ones, and their wives took they captive, and spoiled even all that was in the house.

GEN 49:5 Simeon and Levi are brethren; instruments of cruelty are in their habitations. 6 O my soul, come not thou into their secret; unto their assembly, mine honour, be not thou united: for in their anger, they slew a man, and in their self-will they digged down a wall. 7 Cursed be their anger, for it was fierce; and their wrath, for it was cruel: I will divide them in Jacob, and scatter them in Israel.

Levi, The Third Son

Levi had a choice. He could follow the crowd as he followed Simeon, or he could be the divine communicator. Levi was called out to be the voice of the people to God and the voice of God to the people.

Of the tribe of Levi, Moses was chosen to communicate between God and Israel. In turn, Moses asked God to choose a man to speak to the Pharaoh for Moses. God called Aaron, his brother, another Levite. Levites are showmen and at the center of attention at the ceremonies of the Lord. Levites were arrayed in "show garments", robes and ephods. They were taken care of by the tithes of the people. Levites owned no land and were not counted in the census. Of all numbers, 3 and 7 are used most as holy numbers. It is no wonder that the third son is chosen to serve the Lord.

GEN 29:34 And she conceived again, and bare a son; and said, now this time will my husband be joined unto me, because I have born him three sons: therefore was his name called Levi.

EXO 2:1 And there went a man of the house of Levi, and took to wife a daughter of Levi. 2 And the woman conceived, and bare a son: and when she saw him that he was a goodly child, she hid him three months. 3 And when she could no longer hide him, she took for him an ark of bulrushes, and daubed it with slime and with pitch, and put the child therein; and she laid it in the flags by the river's brink. 4 And his sister stood afar off, to wit what would be done to him. 5 And the daughter of Pharaoh came down to wash herself at the river; and her maidens walked along by the river's side; and when she saw the ark among the flags, she sent her maid to fetch it. 6 And when she had opened it, she saw the child: and, behold, the babe wept. And she had compassion on him, and said, this is one of the Hebrews' children. 7 Then said his sister to Pharaoh's daughter, shall I go and call to thee a nurse of the Hebrew women, that she may nurse the child for thee? 8 and Pharaoh's daughter said to her, Go. And the maid went and called the child's mother. 9 And Pharaoh's daughter said unto her, take this child away, and nurse it for me, and I will give thee thy wages. And the woman took the child, and nursed it. 10 And the child grew, and she brought him unto Pharaoh's daughter, and he became her son. And she called his name Moses: and she said, Because I drew him out of the water.

NUM 1:49 Only thou shalt not number the tribe of Levi, neither take the sum of them among the children of Israel: 50 But thou shalt appoint the Levites over the tabernacle of testimony, and over all the vessels thereof, and over all things that belong to it: they shall bear the tabernacle, and all the vessels thereof; and they shall minister unto it, and shall encamp round about the tabernacle.

NUM 17:8 And it came to pass, that on the morrow Moses went into the tabernacle of witness; and, behold, the rod of Aaron for the house of Levi was budded, and brought forth buds, and bloomed blossoms, and yielded almonds.

DEU 31:9 And Moses wrote this law, and delivered it unto the priests the sons of Levi, which bare the ark of the covenant of the LORD, and unto all the elders of Israel.

Judah, The Fourth Son

Judah was stubborn and driven. He was fundamental in his judgment and quick to forgive. He was "earthy" and genuine as a person. He saw his faults when they were pointed out. Judah is the foundation and root from which our Christian faith springs. Jesus is called the Lion of Judah. This tribe was given the promise of the Law and Scepter. God considered them solid and reliable.

GEN 29:35 And she conceived again, and bare a son: and she said, now will I praise the LORD: therefore she called his name Judah; and left bearing. Judah, thou art he whom thy brethren shall praise: thy hand shall be in the neck of thine enemies; thy father's children shall bow down before thee. Judah is a lion's whelp: from the prey, my son, thou art gone up: he stooped down, he couched as a lion, and as an old lion; who shall rouse him up? The scepter shall not depart from Judah, nor a lawgiver from between his feet, until Shiloh come; and unto him shall the gathering of the people be. Binding his foal unto the vine, and his ass's colt unto the choice vine; he washed his garments in wine, and his clothes in the blood of grapes: His eyes shall be red with wine, and his teeth white with milk.

GEN 37:26 And Judah said unto his brethren, what profit is it if we slay our brother, and conceal his blood? 27 Come, and let us sell him to the Ishmaelites, and let not our hand be upon him; for he is our brother and our flesh. And his brethren were content.

GEN 38:13 And it was told Tamar, saying, behold thy father in law goeth up to Timnath to shear his sheep. 14 And she put her widow's garments off from her, and covered her with a veil, and wrapped herself, and sat in an open place, which is by the way to Timnath; for she saw that Shelah was grown, and she was not given unto him to wife. 15 When Judah saw her, he thought her to be a harlot; because she had covered her face. 16 And he turned unto her by the way, and said, go to, I pray thee, let me come in unto thee; (for he knew not that she was his daughter in law.) And she said, what wilt thou give me, that thou mayest come in unto me? 17 And he said, I will send thee a kid from the flock. And she said, wilt thou give me a pledge, till thou send it? 18 And he said, what pledge shall I give thee? And she said, thy signet, and thy bracelets, and thy staff that is in thine hand. And he gave it her, and came in unto her, and she conceived by him. 19 And she arose, and went away, and laid by her veil from her, and put on the garments of her widowhood.

20 And Judah sent the kid by the hand of his friend the Adullamite, to receive his pledge from the woman's hand: but he found her not. 21 Then he asked the men of that place, saying, where is the harlot, that was openly by the wayside? And they said, there was no harlot in this place. 22 And he returned to Judah, and said, I cannot find her; and also the

men of the place said, that there was no harlot in this place. And Judah said, let her take it to her, lest we be shamed: behold, I sent this kid, and thou hast not found her. 24 And it came to pass about three months after, that it was told Judah, saying, Tamar thy daughter in law hath played the harlot; and also, behold, she is with child by whoredom. And Judah said, bring her forth, and let her be burnt. 25 When she was brought forth, she sent to her father in law, saying, by the man, whose these are, am I with child: and she said, discern, I pray thee, whose are these, the signet, and bracelets, and staff. And Judah acknowledged them, and said, she hath been more righteous than I; because that I gave her not to Shelah my son. And he knew her again no more.

Dan, The Fifth Son

Quixotic and reckless, Dan is quick to turn and quick to strike. The tribe turned to idols and gold. They turned to the sea and stayed in ships. They were spies and artisans; idol worshippers and warriors. They sought earthly wisdom and pleasure and turned away from God. They were seduced by the things of this world.

GEN 30:6 And Rachel said, God hath judged me, and hath also heard my voice, and hath given me a son: therefore called she his name Dan.

GEN 49:16 Dan shall judge his people, as one of the tribes of Israel. 17 Dan shall be a serpent by the way, an adder in the path that biteth the horse heels, so that his rider shall fall backward. 18 I have waited for thy salvation, O LORD.

DEU 33:22 And of Dan he said, Dan is a lion's whelp: he shall leap from Bashan.

EXO 38:23 And with him was Aholiab, son of Ahisamach, of the tribe of Dan, an engraver, and a cunning workman, and an embroiderer in blue, and in purple, and in scarlet, and fine linen. 24 All the gold that was occupied for the work in all the work of the holy place, even the gold of the offering, was twenty and nine talents, and seven hundred and thirty shekels, after the shekel of the sanctuary.

JOS 19:47 And the coast of the children of Dan went out too little for them: therefore the children of Dan went up to fight against Leshem, and took it, and smote it with the edge of the sword, and possessed it, and dwelt therein, and called Leshem, Dan, after the name of Dan their father.

JDG 5:17 Gilead abode beyond Jordan: and why did Dan remain in ships? Asher continued on the sea shore, and abode in his breaches.

Naphtali, The Sixth Son

Naphtali was a servant and a worker. He was a good man, blessed by God. He was a family man who took care of his widowed mother and cared for his family and king.

GEN 30:8 And Rachel said, with great wrestlings have I wrestled with my sister, and I have prevailed: and she called his name Naphtali.

GEN 49:21 Naphtali is a hind let loose: he giveth goodly words.

DEU 33:23 And of Naphtali he said, O Naphtali, satisfied with favor, and full with the blessing of the LORD: possess thou the west and the south.

JDG 5:18 Zebulun and Naphtali were a people that jeoparded their lives unto the death in the high places of the field.

1KI 7:14 He was a widow's son of the tribe of Naphtali, and his father was a man of Tyre, a worker in brass: and he was filled with wisdom, and understanding, and cunning to work all works in brass. And he came to king Solomon, and wrought all his work.

Gad, The Seventh Son

In the day of Gad, the lawgiver was the man of letters who knew the scripture and the law. He was a man of learning. He was part priest and part judge. These men were held in high esteem because of their knowledge of the laws of God. Gad was wealthy, polished, and learned. Yet, there was a place where all of the teachings failed him and he turned from God. In the long run, knowledge never became wisdom. Gad, a troop shall overcome him: but he shall overcome at the last.

GEN 30:9 When Leah saw that she had left bearing, she took Zilpah her maid, and gave her Jacob to wife.10 And Zilpah Leah's maid bare Jacob a son.11 And Leah said, A troop cometh: and she called his name Gad.

NUM 32:1 Now the children of Reuben and the children of Gad had a very great multitude of cattle: and when they saw the land of Jazer, and the land of Gilead, that, behold, the place was a place for cattle.

DEU 33:20 And of Gad he said, Blessed be he that enlargeth Gad: he dwelleth as a lion, and teareth the arm with the crown of the head.21 And he provided the first part for himself, because there, in a portion of the lawgiver, was he seated; and he came with the heads of the people, he executed the justice of the LORD, and his judgments with Israel.

JOS 22:25 For the LORD hath made Jordan a border between us and you, ye children of Reuben and children of Gad; ye have no part in the LORD: so shall your children make our children cease from fearing the LORD.

Asher, The Eighth Son

Asher enjoyed the finer things of life; Royal dainties and rich bread. He dwelt on the seashores. We can speculate that trading and mercantile wealth, and the things money can bring were the reason for his decision. Out of Asher his bread shall be fat, and he shall yield royal dainties.

GEN 30:13 And Leah said, Happy am I, for the daughters will call me blessed: and she called his name Asher.

DEU 33:24 And of Asher he said, Let Asher be blessed with children; let him be acceptable to his brethren, and let him dip his foot in oil.

JDG 5:17 Gilead abode beyond Jordan: and why did Dan remain in ships? Asher continued on the sea shore, and abode in his breaches.

Issachar, The Ninth Son

In Issachar we have the first mention of servitude. The land was good enough. His life was tolerable, so he remained in place... in a day to day existence. Issachar is a symbol of how we pay for our life in the energy, time, or simple endurance of a daily burden. If we do not take note, we will have lived out our lives in servitude to conditions that are only tolerable, and seldom wonderful. Omri is mentioned as a son of Issachar. It bears noting that Omri was the king in Samaria to the ten tribes of the split kingdom of Judah and Israel. The ten tribes were in the second best place, serving in a secondary temple, worshipping an Idol set up by a king not descended from David. They remained in this condition until taken captive. In life, many times it is time that takes us captive without us realizing it until it is too late.

GEN 49:14 Issachar is a strong ass couching (crouching or lying down) down between two burdens (sheepfolds or saddlebags): 15 And he saw that rest was good, and the land that it was pleasant; and bowed his shoulder to bear, and became a servant unto tribute.

GEN 30:17 And God hearkened unto Leah, and she conceived, and bare Jacob the fifth son. 18 And Leah said, God hath given me my hire, because I have given my maiden to my husband: and she called his name Issachar.

1CH 12:32 And of the children of Issachar, which were men that had understanding of the times, to know what Israel ought to do; the heads of them were two hundred; and all their brethren were at their commandment.

1CH 27:18 Of Judah, Elihu, one of the brethren of David: of Issachar, Omri the son of Michael:

Zebulun, The Tenth Son

The tribe of Zebulun was a strong and directed people. They were not afraid. They were writers and scholars. To write and handle the pen put one in a superior position at this time.

Scribes were in a high position in ancient societies. Books were copied and knowledge was a means to influence, persuasion, and control. Scriptures were checked and re-checked. The number of letters in a line were counted and verified. Each page was proofread. All scriptures were copied word for word. Scribes were perfectionists. The faithfulness of the transmission of the word of God depended on the precision of the scribe. Letters were drawn in a codified but artistic fashion. Their work was respected and admired.

GEN 30:20 And Leah said, God hath endued me with a good dowry; now will my husband dwell with me, because I have born him six sons: and she called his name Zebulun. Zebulun shall dwell at the haven of the sea; and he shall be for a haven of ships; and his border shall be unto Zidon.

DEU 33:17 His glory is like the firstling of his bullock, and his horns are like the horns of unicorns: with them he shall push the people together to the ends of the earth: and they are the ten thousands of Ephraim, and they are the thousands of Manasseh. 18 And of Zebulun he said, Rejoice, Zebulun, in thy going out; and, Issachar, in thy tents.

JDG 5:14 Out of Ephraim was there a root of them against Amalek; after thee, Benjamin, among thy people; out of Machir came down governors, and out of Zebulun they that handle the pen of the writer.

1CH 12:33 Of Zebulun, such as went forth to battle, expert in war, with all instruments of war, fifty thousand, which could keep rank: they were not of double heart.

DEU 33:18 And of Zebulun he said, Rejoice, Zebulun, in thy going out; and, Issachar, in thy tents. 19 They shall call the people unto the mountain; there they shall offer sacrifices of righteousness: for they shall suck of the abundance of the seas, and of treasures hid in the sand.

Joseph, The Eleventh Son

A vision is called a dream by those who do not see. The name "Joseph" means "to add." To add to this world takes vision and determination. Joseph saw and believed. He never wavered from his vision. Thus, he believed in his God and his destiny. He rose through the ranks as a politician, statesman, and leader. Even when tempted to do the wrong thing, Joseph held to his ideals and vision.

GEN 49:26 Even by the God of thy father, who shall help thee; and by the Almighty, who shall bless thee with blessings of heaven above, blessings of the deep that lieth under, blessings of the breasts, and of the womb. The blessings of thy father have prevailed above the blessings of my progenitors unto the utmost bound of the everlasting hills. They shall be on the head of Joseph, and on the crown of the head of him that was separate from his brethren. 18 And when they saw him afar off, even before he came near unto them, they conspired against him to slay him. 19 And they said one to another, Behold, this dreamer cometh. 20 Come now therefore, and let us slay him, and cast him into some pit, and we will say, some evil beast hath devoured him: and we shall see what will become of his dreams.

GEN 39:1 And Joseph was brought down to Egypt; and Potiphar, an officer of Pharaoh, captain of the guard, an Egyptian, bought him of the hands of the Ishmaelites, which had brought him down thither. 2 And the LORD was with Joseph, and he was a prosperous man; and he was in the house of his master the Egyptian.3 And his master saw that the LORD was with him, and that the LORD made all that he did to prosper in his hand. 4 And Joseph found grace in his sight, and he served him: and he made him overseer over his house, and all that he had he put into his hand. 5 And it came to pass from the time that he had made him overseer in his house, and over all that he had, that the LORD blessed the Egyptian's house for Joseph's sake; and the blessing of the LORD was upon all that he had in the house, and in the field. 6 And he left all that he had in Joseph's hand; and he knew not ought he had, save the bread which he did eat. And Joseph was a goodly person, and well favored.

DEU 33:13 And of Joseph he said, Blessed of the LORD be his land, for the precious things of heaven, for the dew, and for the deep that coucheth beneath,14 And for the precious fruits brought forth by the sun, and for the precious things put forth by the moon, 15 And for the chief things of the ancient mountains, and for the precious things of the lasting hills,16 And for the precious things of the earth and fullness thereof, and for the good will of him that dwelt in the bush: let the blessing come upon the head of Joseph, and upon the top of the head of him that was separated from his brethren.

Benjamin, The Twelfth Son

When it came to training and warfare, the tribe of Benjamin was more machine than man. They were left handed or could fight equally with both left and right. They were perfection in motion. Seven hundred chosen men of Benjamin were left-handed and everyone could sling stones at a "hair breadth", and not miss. They looked at training as formula, system, and science. This tribe spawned King Saul. The king was appointed by God, anointed by a priest, and was insane in the end. This type has the ability to be leader and king but struggles with the ability to contain and express conflicting emotions. Benjamin's people were prophesied to be powerful and successful if they could temper their tendency to "ravin" – "be violent, greedy, or to devourer greedily." Benjamin represents the highest and lowest that man alone can achieve. King or lunatic, conqueror or madman, science, or fanaticism, it is all decided in the spiritual balance.

GEN 49:27 Benjamin shall ravin as a wolf: in the morning he shall devour the prey, and at night he shall divide the spoil. 28 All these are the twelve tribes of Israel: and this is it that their father spake unto them, and blessed them; every one according to his blessing he blessed them.

DEU 33:12 And of Benjamin he said, the beloved of the LORD shall dwell in safety by him; and the Lord shall cover him all the day long, and he shall dwell between his shoulders.

JDG 20: 14 But the children of Benjamin gathered themselves together out of the cities unto Gibeah, to go out to battle against the children of Israel. 15 And the children of Benjamin were numbered at that time out of the cities twenty and six thousand men that drew sword, beside the inhabitants of Gibeah, which were numbered seven hundred chosen men. 16 Among all this people there were seven hundred chosen men left-handed; everyone could sling stones at a hair breadth, and not miss. 17 And the men of Israel, beside Benjamin, were numbered four hundred thousand men that drew sword: all these were men of war.

2CH 34:32 And he caused all that were present in Jerusalem and Benjamin to stand to it. And the inhabitants of Jerusalem did according to the covenant of God, the God of their fathers. 33 And Josiah took away all the abominations out of all the countries that pertained to the children of Israel, and made all that were present in Israel to serve, even to serve the LORD their God. And all his days they departed not from following the LORD, the God of their fathers.

1SA 11:15 And all the people went to Gilgal; and there they made Saul. 14 But now thy kingdom shall not continue: the LORD hath sought him a man after his own heart, and the LORD hath commanded him to be captain over his people, because thou hast not kept that which the LORD commanded thee.

The personality types found in the sons and tribes of Jacob may have been used to augment and expand Gurdjieff's understanding of the developing Enneagram. Could it be that the authors of the Enneagram began its catalog of insights into human nature from the attributes seen in the men of the tribes of Jacob? As the knowledge contained in the Enneagram is re-ordered and combined with the qualities of the twelve tribes, we shall see a rich and deep mosaic describing human personality and human nature.

There are two items that must be pointed out before we begin to address the Enneagram types and compare them to the ancient sources we have described.

1) The ancients believed a person was what they did. They were not concerned with why. Types in the ancient world were about actions. Types within the Enneagram are based on motives and motivations.

2) The Enneagram 5 corresponds to the Numerology 7 and the Enneagram 7 corresponds to the Numerology 5. It really does not matter what the Enneagram types are called since numbers are simply used as handles or tag names.

Sufis and the Mystic Numbers

Sufism was a liberal reform movement within Islam. Sufism was a push or reaction to free Islam from its legalism and place it on a more internal and mystical path. It had its origin in Persia and spread into India in the 11th century.

Just as Christianity has its mystical tradition, which seems to transcend denomination in its search for "the heart of God", so Islam has its mystical branch. These are the Sufis.

Sufism is a search for divine love and truth through direct personal connection with God. The tradition began in a form of asceticism, based on the teachings of Hasan al-Basri. Followers sought the experience of divine love, as taught by al-Ghazali and Attar of Nishapur. The movement has been refined into a religious order based on the teachings of Sufis such as Rumi and Yunus Emre. Its purpose is to rid oneself of ego and experience the directly attainable love of God. Since it is a mystical order, there are meditations and mystical beliefs and practices. Numbers play a role in this. It is believed by many that Gurdjieff gained many of his insights from Sufi numerology before developing his theories, which formed the basis of the Enneagram.

The reasoning of Sufi mystics holds that numbers are infinite in both directions. Infinitely large and infinitely small. God will always distance himself from the seeker by the next order of number. If we come to understand all there is to the number 101, God will move to 102. Likewise, if man understands the infinitesimal, such as .001 nanometers, God will be at .0001. Thus we will always chase God but never fully obtain him.

Numbers are created within our imagination. Creation itself sprang from the imagination of God. Imagination is light and is divine. Its use can perform good or evil.

1 – One is the number of unity and God. Each number is created by adding 1, thus it is a creative force and is not considered a number. One is Alif, the Divine Essence. The line with no beginning and no end.

2 - Two is the number of this realm. It is the number of opposing forces. Things were created in duality. Light and dark, hot and cold, male and female… Two is the number of distress and the dynamic tension within this realm.

3 - Three is the first odd number. It is the number of equilibrium since 3 legs can be stable. Three is the number of creation. Three stands for the way things in this realm manifest. It is the essence of a thing plus the energy of creation that brings about the form so it can be known. Three is the number of affection plus reason resulting in divine creation.

4 – Four is the number of authority and the prophets of God. Four is the number of loyalty. In Islam, a man may have 4 wives. The fourth month stands for vigor, energy, and youth. Because 1+2+4+4=10 it is said that perfection is reached in four.

5 - Five is the balance point and the place where all other numbers are maintained. Five is the number of prayer and being mindful of things and of God. There are five Pillars of Islam, Call to Belief, Prayer, Almsgiving, Fasting/abstaining, and Migration to the Divine.

6 - Six is the number of completion and perfection. God made the world in six days and it was perfect. According to a certain tradition, the sixth step toward perfecting the world for Allah is for the prophet to cleanse the earth (of non-believers) and make the entire world a mosque. This would make the world a home for God.

7 – Seven is the peak of perfection. The holy day. There are seven planets. (In the time of the writing of this wisdom the outer planets were not known.) Seven is the connecting of God's wisdom to his people. According to esoteric readings,

Seven people are in the highest position of spiritual authority over the people. Four of them are main posts, two are poles and one is a saint. Through these people, God governs his people and the universe.

8 – Eight is eternity. It is the throne and the one who sits upon it. It is the number of praise.

9 – Nine, the 9th attribute of Allah is the one who compels. The ninth name is the Freer of hellfire. Nine is the end. It ends all numbers before the new order begins. Nine months ends the human gestation and life here begins. It is the end of a cycle.

There are other sacred numbers within Sufism.

10 – Every ten years of a human life has a different characteristic. There are ten years for each stage of life.

12 - There are twelve constellations. Twelve is the number of precision and surety of movement.

14 - The number of separated (mukattaa) letters in the Qur'an is 14. The forming of these letters at the beginning of the chapter (sura) denotes the names of angels. These angels are called by reading these letters. These angels are charged to protect the reader from the negative energies in the time being read. The letters or disjointed letters or disconnected letters are combinations of between one and five Arabic letters figuring at the beginning of 29 out of the 114 chapters (surahs) of the Quran. They have been interpreted as abbreviations for either names or qualities of God or for the names or content of the respective chapters (surahs).

28 - Twice 14 and the second perfect number.

33 – There are 33 prayer beads. It is the highest spiritual state man can achieve.

70 – The mercy of God. The number of "repents". Unlimited multiplicity.

Origins of the System

We're going to look at G.I. Gurdjieff, but with a caveat. Even though Gurdjieff is said to be the father of the Enneagram, he is not. Like many findings in the 19th century, the initial use of Gurdjieff's system was metaphysical in nature and not focused on personality or reinforced by empirical data. Instead, his work merely laid the philosophical foundation for the Enneagram we use today. Nonetheless, Gurdjieff was a truly noteworthy character of his time. Exploration of his life and the metaphysical "scaffolding" that laid the groundwork of the enneagram will further our understanding of the modern enneagram we see in action today.

George Ivanovich Gurdjieff (Geórgy Ivánovich Gurdzhíev), c. 1866–1877 – 29 October 1949) Gurdjieff was an Armenian philosopher, mystic, composer, and spiritual leader. He was born in Alexandropol, in the old Russian Empire. The city is now known as Gyumri, Armenia. Gurdjieff was born to Yiannis Georgiades, a Greek man from the Caucasus region, and an Armenian mother, Evdokia.

Armenia is a landlocked country in Western Asia. It is a part of the Caucasus region; and is bordered by Turkey to the west, Georgia to the north, Azerbaijan to the east, and Iran to the south. Remember that Chaldia, the origin of Chaldean

Numerology, was bounded to the north by the Black Sea, to the east by Lazica, the westernmost part of Caucasian Iberia, to the south by the Kurdish region of Turkey and what the Romans and Byzantines called Armenia Minor, and to the west by the western half of Pontus. Pontus is a region located in the modern-day eastern Black Sea Region of Turkey. This is important because it gave Gurdjieff access to the regional knowledge that could have contained Chaldean Numerology.

The exact year of his birth remains unknown. James Moore argued for 1866. Gurdjieff's secretary in the early 1930s, Louise Goepfert March, and the woman who he called the first friend of his inner life, Olga de Hartmann, believed he was born in 1872. He once stated that he was born at the beginning of New Year's Day, but his passport stated he was born on November 28, 1877. The year 1872 is written on the grave marker in the cemetery of Avon, Seine-et-Marne, France, where he was buried. It should be noted that since Gurdjieff's father was Greek, it is possible Gurdjieff could have been exposed to the teaching of the great Greek philosophers, including Pythagoras, from a young age.

Gurdjieff thought most people lack a unified consciousness. Instead, he believed people live in a state of hypnotic "waking sleep". He believed it was possible to awaken and thus reach a higher state of consciousness. He believed becoming fully awake was the only way to achieve full human potential. Gurdjieff described his method of awakening as a discipline he called "The Work" (connoting "work on oneself") or "the System".

"The Work" is essentially training to develop one's consciousness. Gurdjieff used a variety of methods to teach his students, including meetings, music, sacred dances, writings, lectures, and many other unorthodox forms of group and individual work. The function of these various methods was to challenge and alter the established patterns of the mind and encourage moments of deep insight. Gurdjieff knew each student had various personal needs, and did not adopt one uniform method of teaching, rather he adjusted and innovated to accommodate each student's specific situation. In Russia he was known for restricting his teaching to very small groups, whereas in Paris, as well as in North America, he did many larger public presentations.

Gurdjieff thought that the typical approaches of self-knowledge—those of the fakir, monk, and yogi (practiced through discomfort, commitment, and study, respectively)—were insufficient by themselves and frequently resulted in different types of stagnancies or one-sidedness. He designed his methodology in an effort to combine and change the traditional thereby speeding up the developmental process.

He coined his methods "The Way of the Sly Man" because he saw them as a short-cut through the development process that otherwise could carry on for many years without any impactful results. The experienced teacher knows the individual needs of each disciple and challenges them in ways that he knows will transform each student's consciousness, individually. Parallels can be found in the teachings of Zen Buddhism, where teachers used a variety of methods, some very unorthodox, to prompt the arising of insight in the student.

Gurdjieff often said his methodology for awakening one's consciousness was a holistic amalgamation of methods from the fakir, monk, and yogi, greater than the sum of its parts, and thus referred to it as the "Fourth Way".

Fakir is a traditional Islamic term used to describe Sufi Muslim ascetics who renounce worldly possessions and dedicate their lives to the worship of Allah (God). They shun the adornments of the material and worldly life that detract from their constant dedication to God. They acknowledge their spiritual neediness and dedicate themselves to prayer and devotional practices, which consists of repeating the names of God with various rituals. It is not common knowledge that these saints use numerology in their meditative studies.

In a paper presented in London to The Temenos Academy at the Royal Asiatic Society,

London on July 8, 2008, titled, "Abjad: the Numerological Language of Spiritual Insight and Guidance as Employed in Sufism", Robert Abdul Hayy Darr is quoted as saying,

"Sufi teaching, including the use of numerology, is only helpful, however, if it truly enables us to transcend the illusion of individual separateness, because it is this illusion which prevents us from realizing our true, divine origins. Interest in esoteric teachings can be hazardous to genuine spiritual study if people turn to them craving personal power or special knowledge that others do not have. This kind of fascination with esoteric terminology only reinforces egocentricity. We must bear this hazard in mind if we are to correctly approach esoteric teachings like numerology."

Gurdjieff also drew on esoteric knowledge and studied the works of the Desert Fathers, a group of Christian mystics. One of the Desert Fathers in particular, Evagrius Ponticus, was highly influential to Gurdjieff when developing "The Work." Gurdjieff himself referred to Ponticus' teachings as "esoteric Christianity."

Gurdjieff identified himself as Pythagorean Greek and a Gnostic Christian. Both of these groups put great value in numbers both as symbols and guideposts of hidden knowledge within holy texts.

Gurdjieff is famous for taking great measures in concealing the sources of his knowledge and teaching, never disclosing them even to his closest students. His secrecy has given rise to great speculation as to where he acquired the knowledge for his teachings. Students of Gurdjieff and certain scholars have identified many influences in Gurdjieff's teachings including Christian mysticism, sects of Muslim Sufis, Buddhism, Hinduism and Pythagorean traditions, but certain aspects of his teachings are unique and cannot be traced back to any known literature.

Gurdjieff spent his early years in Kars, the capital of the Kars Oblast region, a location in modern day Turkey which existed as a Russian territory from 1878 to 1917. Kars was a border region that, at the time, Russia had recently captured from the Ottoman Empire. It contained an extensive grassy plateau-steppe, high mountains and was inhabited by a diverse group of people and faiths. The people respected the traveling mystics and holy men that passed through. The city and surrounding areas were home to Armenians, Russians, Caucasus Greeks, Georgians, Turks, Kurds and smaller numbers of Christian communities from eastern and central Europe such as Caucasus Germans, and Estonians.

Gurdjieff takes particular interest in the Yazidi community. Yazidis are native to Kurdistan, a region in Western Asia that includes parts of modern Iraq, Syria, Turkey, and Iran. Yazidi people are a distinct ethnoreligious group that are monotheistic in nature, having roots that predate the Zoroastrian faith. Yazidism is a monotheistic faith based on belief in one God, who created the world and entrusted it into the care of seven Holy Beings, called the Seven Mysteries). The head of these beings is Tawûsê Melek / Melek Taûs, the Peacock Angel.

Growing up in an ethnically diverse society, Gurdjieff became fluent in Armenian, Greek, Russian and Turkish. He later became conversant in several European languages. In his youth, Gurdjieff read Russian-language scientific literature. He was influenced by these writings; it is possible the influence of these books, along with the fact he witnessed a number of phenomena that he could not explain, gave way to his strong conviction that there existed truths hidden from and unexplored by science or in mainstream religion.

In early adulthood, Gurdjieff's curiosity led him to travel to Central Asia, Egypt, Iran, India, Tibet and Rome. He returned to Russia in 1912. He then wrote a memoir in which he stated that he had met remarkable men and "seekers of truth", in which he spoke and wrote of encounters with dervishes, fakirs and descendants of the extinct Essenes. He claimed their teaching had been conserved at a monastery in Sarmoung. The Sarmoung Brotherhood was a group of mystics who preserved the original teaching of Zoroaster. Many believe they are fictitious. Much of Gurdjieff's book was considered allegorical in nature and not a true history of his travels.

If the list of places he had traveled are correct, Gurdjieff would have encountered the ancient repositories of Sufi, Chaldean, Vedic, Pythagorean, Egyptian, and other mystical schools, all of which had their own brands of numerology.

Remember, Gurdjieff believed people cannot accurately perceive reality in their current condition because they do not possess a unified consciousness but instead live in a state of a hypnotic "waking sleep".

"Man lives his life in sleep, and in sleep he dies." As a result, each person perceives the world from a completely subjective perspective. He asserted that people typically function as unconscious automatons, but that one can "wake up" and become a different kind of human being altogether.

Some modern researchers claim Gurdjieff's concept of self-remembering is similar to the Buddhist concept of awareness or today's usage of 'mindfulness.' The terms come from the

Pali term sati, which is identical to Sanskrit smṛti meaning to remember.

Gurdjieff claimed that many existing religions and forms of spirituality had lost connection with their original meaning and could no longer serve humanity in the way was originally intended. As a result, humans were failing to find the truths the ancient teachings offer and were instead becoming more like automatons, susceptible to influence from outside forces and increasingly capable of terrible acts induced by mass psychosis such as World War I. The surviving schools of thought only provided one-sided development, which did not result in a fully integrated human being.

According to Gurdjieff, only one of the three dimensions of a person — the emotions, the physical body, or the mind — tends to develop in such schools and sects, and commonly at the expense of other faculties or "centers." As a result, these paths do not form a properly balanced human being. Furthermore, anyone wishing to undertake any of the traditional paths to spiritual knowledge was required to renounce life in the world. Gurdjieff's observations led him to develop the "Fourth Way" which would accommodate the requirements of people living in modern Europe and America. Gurdjieff's way focused on all three facets of human wisdom, mind, body, and emotion, to promote comprehensive and balanced inner development.

Gurdjieff's way sought to answer the question of humanity's place in the universe and the importance of developing latent potential within each person, which can be defined as our natural endowment as human beings, though few of us are able to bring this to fruition. He taught that higher levels of consciousness, inner growth, and holistic development are attainable, but require a great amount of conscious work to achieve.

Gurdjieff gave very distinct meanings to various ancient texts including the Bible and many religious prayers and practices. He believed these texts held very different meanings from those commonly attributed to them. Passages including *sleep not; awake, for you know not the hour;* and *the kingdom of heaven is within* are all examples of biblical statements that had lost their original meaning over time.

Gurdjieff taught people how to maximize attention and energy in various ways and minimize absentmindedness. According to his teaching, inner development of self is the beginning of a possible greater process of change, the aim of which is to transform people into what they ought to be.

Gurdjieff distrusted morality, describing it as varying between cultures and often contradictory. Instead, he stressed the importance of one's conscience.

Gurdjieff also taught his pupils "sacred dances" or "movements" as a method of focusing on inner attention more intensively. Later these became known as the Gurdjieff movements, which they performed together as a group. He also left a body of music written for piano in collaboration with his pupil Thomas de Hartmann. The body of works was inspired by what he heard during visits to remote monasteries and other places.

Gurdjieff also used various exercises, such as the "Stop" exercise, to promote the practice of self-observation in his students. He practiced many shock tactics to help awaken his pupils from constant daydreaming and these shocks were always possible at any moment

P.D Oupensky briefly describes the stop exercise in his book In Search of the Miraculous:

> Soon after that G. began to put "stop," as we called this exercise, into practice in the most varied circumstances. G. first of all showed us how to "stand stock-still" immediately at the command "stop," and to try not to move, not to look aside no matter what was happening,

not to reply if anyone spoke, for instance if one were asked something or even unjustly accused of something.

"The 'stop' exercise is considered sacred in schools," he said. "Nobody except the principal teacher or the person he commissions has the right to command a 'stop.' 'Stop' cannot be the subject of play or exercise among the pupils. You never know the position a man can find himself in. If you cannot feel for him, you do not know what muscles are tensed or how much. Meanwhile, if a difficult tension is continued it can cause the rupture of some important vessel and in some cases, it can even cause immediate death. Therefore, only he who is quite certain that he knows what he is doing can allow himself to command a 'stop.'

"At the same time 'stop' demands unconditional obedience, without any hesitations or doubts."

P.D Ouspensky, also known as Pyotr Demianovich Ouspenskii or Peter D Ouspensky, was one of Gurdjieff's chief students for some 25 years. Ouspensky was a Russian born man known as a scientist, mathematician, and for his study of esoteric knowledge. He is primarily known for his expositions on Gurdjieff's teaching, which he recounts in his books *In Search of the Miraculous*, *The Fourth Way*, and *The*

Tertium Organum. The *Tertium Organum* was published before he met Gurdjieff and is widely renowned as an influential philosophical work. The *Tertium Organum*, also known as the third canon of philosophical thought, is widely considered the third great philosophical work, the first two being the works of Aristotle and Frances Bacon. He has been associated with Gurdjieff's teaching and practices since 1915 when he met Gurdjieff in Moscow. He is known to have taught ideas from the Gurdjieff system in England and the United States for some 25 years before personally separating himself from Gurdjieff in 1924.

In response to political changes in Georgia and the crumbling of the old Georgian order, Gurdjieff and his party left Georgia in late spring of 1920 for Batumi on the Black Sea coast and shortly after traveled by ship to Istanbul. Gurdjieff rented an apartment on Kumbaracı Street in Péra and later moved to 13 Abdullatif Yemenici Sokak near the Galata Tower. The apartment is near the khanqah (monastery) of the Mevlevi Order (a Sufi Order following the teachings of Jalal al-Din Muhammad Rumi), where Gurdjieff, Ouspensky and Thomas de Hartmann witnessed the sema ceremony of the Whirling Dervishes. Gurdjieff also met Capt. John G. Bennett, head of British Military Intelligence in Constantinople at the time.

Captain Bennett described his impression of Gurdjieff this way:

> It was there that I first met Gurdjieff in the autumn of 1920, and no surroundings could have been more appropriate. In Gurdjieff, East and West do not just meet. Their difference is annihilated in a world outlook which knows no distinctions of race or creed. This was my first and has remained one of my strongest impressions. A Greek from the Caucasus, he spoke Turkish with an accent of unexpected purity, the accent that one associates with those born and bred in the narrow circle of the Imperial Court. His appearance was striking enough even in Turkey, where one saw many unusual types. His head was shaven, immense black moustache, eyes which at one moment seemed very pale and at another almost black. Below average height, he gave nevertheless an impression of great physical strength.

Gurdjieff and his followers arrived in Constantinople on July 7, 1920.

Ouspensky decided to work with Gurdjieff again and turned over his pupils. Ouspensky gave lectures at Gurdjieff's Institute in Constantinople at the time. Sometime in the spring of 1921 Ouspensky noticed that Gurdjieff seemed to be going out of his way to insight arguments and misunderstandings. Ouspensky, alarmed by Gurdjieff's behavior, began to consider leaving. The opportunity presented itself in May 1921 when Ouspensky received a telegram from Lady Rothermere. Impressed with Ouspensky's book, *Tertium Organum*, she offered to pay all his expenses if he would come to London.

Tertium Organum was written before his encounter with Gurdjieff and is based entirely on his own experiences before he learned about theosophy. Ouspenski developed the concept of the fourth dimension as "a broad metaphor for the esoteric nature of reality." At the time, Einstein and other physicists were validating the study of "other dimensions," and Ouspenski was keenly interested in the topic. His efforts to "experience higher states of consciousness" focused on proving that "modern man needed an entirely new model of accessing knowledge; a qualitatively different mode from the two modes (classical and positivist) that had dominated Western civilization for 2000 years." The *Tertium Organum* takes ideas from the teachings of the mystics of East and West, as well as from sacred art and modern scientific theories. Ouspenski established that the three-dimensional world would be the result of man's limited physical apparatus, with the real world of the three dimensions being a limited projection of that other existential plane of the fourth dimension where man would have a consciousness.

During the same period Ouspensky approached Gurdjieff with his idea to write a book showcasing Gurdjieff's St. Petersburg lectures with Oupensky's own commentaries. Gurdjieff agreed to authorize the publication. In August, Gurdjieff saw conditions were deteriorating in Constantinople and left with a small entourage, including Madame Ouspensky and her family. She had made the choice to study under Gurdjieff rather than Ouspensky. Ouspensky left Constantinople for London in the same month.

Ouspensky studied the Gurdjieff system under Gurdjieff's supervision for a decade, from 1915 to 1924. Ouspensky's book, In Search of the Miraculous, recounts what he learned from Gurdjieff during this time. While lecturing in London in 1924, he announced that he would move forward as an independent scholar the way he had when he left Gurdjieff's supervision in 1921. Some, including a close student named Rodney Collin, state that he renounced the system in 1947, but Gurdjieff's recorded words on the subject ("A Record of Meetings", published posthumously) do not clearly endorse this.

In 1935, Gurdjieff discontinued work on *All and Everything*, the original name for a trilogy he planned to release. He had completed the first two parts of the three-part work, but the third remained unfinished. (It was later published under the title *Life Is Real Only Then, When 'I Am'*.) In 1936, he settled in a home at 6, Rue des Colonels-Renard, Paris, France, where he lived for the remainder of his life. Gurdjieff's brother Dmitry died in 1937, which led to disbandment of The Rope.

The Rope was a small band of exceptional women who learned under Gurdjieff. The women of the Rope included Solita Solano, Kathryn Hulme, Alice Rohrer and Elizabeth Gordon. Solana and Hume quote Gurdjieff's description of The Rope to them as

> "You are going on a journey under my guidance, an 'inner-world journey' like a high mountain climb where you must be roped together for safety, where each must think of the others on the rope, all for one and one for all. You must, in short, help each other 'as hand washes hand,' each contributing to the company according to her lights, according to her means. Only faithful hard work on yourselves will get you where I want you to go, not your wishing."

Gurdjieff never explicitly divulged the sources of his teachings and the origin of the enneagram has been a source of speculation. Some believe that Gurdjieff learned the enneagram from Sufis in Central Asia. This would place him close enough to have encountered wisdom of the Pythagorean teachings, as well as the wisdom of numerics contained in several holy books.

Although it is commonly believed that Oscar Ichazo used ancient wisdom from either Sufi or Christian origins to create his typology of the enneagram, Ichazo himself stated that he created the Enneagram Fixations using Gurdjieff's enneagram as a prototype.

The eight-pointed star of the enneagram was introduced to the West by G.I. Gurdjieff in 1916 as a symbol of the harmonic structure and inner dynamic of the cosmos. Oscar Ichazo's Enneagram of Fixations came out in the 1970s as an application of the enneagram, quite distinct from Gurdjieff's original diagram of the "Law of 3 and 7." Shortly after its release, it was built upon further by Claudio Naranjo in the Seekers After Truth (SAT) groups in Berkeley, CA.

In the writings of Evagrius Ponticus, a Greek Christian contemplative living in the Egyptian desert in the fourth century AD, we may see the origin of the Enneagram. Evagrius' writings show both enneagram- like symbolism and "the 8 evil thoughts," which later became "the 7 deadly sins" of Christianity.

The most notable feature of Evagrius' research was his system of categorizing the different forms of temptation. In AD 375, He developed a comprehensive list of eight evil thoughts (λογισμοὶ, Logismoi), also known as the eight terrible temptations, from which all sinful behavior is born. This list was intended for self-diagnosis: to aid readers as they identify the process of temptation, individual strengths and weaknesses, and various remedies available to overcome temptation.

Evagrius stated "The first thought of all is that of love of self; after this, the eight." In so stating, he set aside the love of self as the first and most pervasive, if not universal, of sins. After this sin comes the eight sins, of which, depending on one's personality, each will suffer at least one main temptation.

The eight patterns of evil thought are **gluttony, lust, greed, sadness, acedia [spiritual or mental despondency or slothfulness], anger, vainglory, and pride.** In 590 AD, Pope Gregory I, also known as "Pope Gregory The Great" would revise this list to form the modern Seven Deadly Sins, where he combined acedia (despondency) with tristitia (sorrow), referring to the combination as the sin of sloth; vainglory combined with pride; and envy was added to the list of "Seven Deadly Sins".

These are clearly seen in the outline of the Enneagram:

1 – Anger / Resentment

2 – Pride

3 – Deceit

4 – Envy

5 – Greed / Avarice

6 – Fear / Anxiety

7 – Gluttony

8 – Lust

9 - Sloth

Evagrius wrote his texts in the fourth century, a critical period in the development of the Christian Church. In 324 AD, Constantine declared Christianity the Roman state religion and as Rome was Christianized, Christianity was Romanized. In typical fashion, the church began to take on a military frame of mind and set about to bring everyone into line. Evagrius would be affected.

Evagrius was known by his followers to have achieved a remarkable degree of harmony with others and himself through monk-like austere practices and prayer. This did not matter to the church. Evagrius had ideas divergent from the mainstream faith at the time. It may have been because he studied the work of Pythagoras, or other pagans as he investigated sacred numbers, or maybe it was simply because he was too far ahead of his time, but the church eventually turned against him. In 399 AD, the same year as his death, his followers were persecuted as heretics and forced into exile. In 553 A.D., 154 years after his death, Evagrius was condemned at the Fifth Ecumenical Council. The venom of the church did not stop there. He would be condemned by the following three Councils as well.

Fortunately, his disciples were able to bring some of his works with them as they were forced in to exile from the Roman Empire. Evagrius' followers spread his work into Armenia and the Arabic world where his works greatly influenced Persian Sufis and Byzantine theologians. His influence and his ideas of a catalog of sins based on various human weaknesses or fixations made their way into the mind of Gurdjieff.

Even though Gurdjieff was probably influenced by the symbol and writings of Evagrius, the source of the symbol was likely Gurdjieff himself. He was fixated on the sacred numbers of one and seven. If these are divided as shown, a pattern emerges that exactly follows the path of the enneagram symbol. We now have the symbol as a modification of Evagrius' work, and a direction of connections taken from the sacred numbers of 1/7 (0.142857142857) upon which Gurdjieff's enneagram symbol is based. Notice the sequence is missing 3,6, and 9, which in the enneagram stand alone in a separate unconnected triangle.

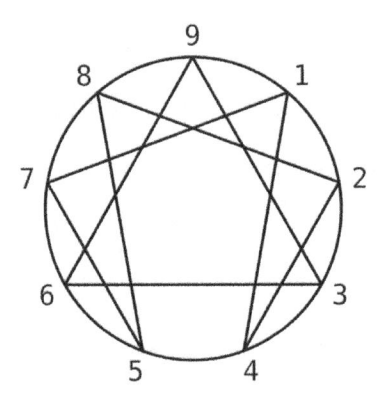

The enneagram figure was later used as a method of personality analysis, principally with the Enneagram of Personality as developed by Oscar Ichazo, Claudio Naranjo and others. Few aspects of the group's application are directly connected to Gurdjieff's system or his use of the Enneagram.

From the Wisdom of Central Asia and the Near East to the writings of the Desert Fathers, Gurdjieff gathered his ideas and produced both a philosophy and a system of self improvement. His ideas were not used by him to type or understand personalities. The symbol and direction of flow were used by others to produce a fully functional personality typing system.

Thus, the "Traditional Enneagram" only goes back to the 1960's when Oscar Ichazo first developed his theory of Ego-Fixation.

Oscar Ichazo developed a system of teachings based on the ancient symbol of the Enneagram. The Enneagram symbol has roots in antiquity and can be traced back to the Desert Fathers. We know that Evagrius studied the work of Pythagoras and had a deep curiosity of sacred numbers. It is believed Evagius designed his symbol based on those of the Pythagoreans. The symbol was reintroduced to the modern world by George Gurdjieff.

Gurdjieff taught the symbol primarily through a series of sacred movements or sacred dances, constructed to give the participant a deep understanding of the symbol and what it represents. It is clear, however, that Gurdjieff did not teach a system of personality types associated with the symbol.

Gurdjieff did reveal to advanced students what he called their chief feature. The chief feature is the foundation or driving force of a person's ego structure. It is a list of basic characteristics that defines them. Gurdjieff generally used rude descriptions of a person's ego features. He would declare people to be round idiots, square idiots, subjective idiot, hopeless idiots, squirming idiots, and so forth. But application to the Enneagram symbol was never discussed.

It was Oscar Ichazo who postulated nine main ways that we lose our center and become distorted in our thinking, feeling, and doing, and are thus the nine ways that we forget our connection with the Divine. These nine fixations drive us away from our divine nature and predispose us to one of nine passions, each attached to a given fixation. A fixation, in the context

Ichazo used the term, can be defined as a strong tendency toward a specific way of being.

The Enneagram According to Óscar Ichazo

The Three Instincts

According to Óscar Ichazo, fixations are birthed from insecurities in one of three fundamental human instincts; Conservation (stemming from the digestive system), Relation (stemming from the circulatory system), and Adaptation (stemming from the nervous system). All people use all three of the instincts at certain times, but each person is predisposed to use one more often than the others. The egos arise from the three instincts: the Historical Ego, the Image Ego, and the Practical Ego. Every individual possesses each of the three egos and conflict between them results in one of nine possible fixations to develop.

Conservation Instinct

The Conservation Instinct is attached to the digestive system and is responsible for conserving physical health and maintaining or attaining physical satisfaction. The Historical Ego comes from this instinct. The Historical Ego holds memories of how and where to get food along with memories of physical states of being. It maintains our sense of daily activities such as sleeping, cooking, walking, eating, etc.

Subconsciously, it constantly asks the question "How am I?" It is concerned with the physical state of the body and sensory information associated with it. It uses comparative reasoning to assess the state things have been in the past and how they will change over time. It is extremely detail oriented and uses this to determine and evaluate the environment around it. This instinct manifests in the mental poison of greed, fed by the need to continually seek more food and lust for material gain in effort to satisfy the digestive system. Greed is then expressed as one of three separate poisons. The first is avarice, which fosters Ego-Vengeance also known as the Over Justice Maker, the second is greed itself, which fosters Ego-Indolence also known as the Over Non Conformist, and the third is possessiveness, which fosters Ego-Resentment also known as the Over Perfectionist.

Relation Instinct

The Relation Instinct is attached to the circulatory system. It determines how we interact with other people and how we establish our individual selves. The Image Ego is derived from this instinct. The Image Ego wants to develop a working self image that fits with society. It is people oriented and questions how people perceive us and how we perceive others by continually asking the question "who am I with." This ego supervises all of our relationships including how we interact with family, friends, and people, including entities with whom we work. It is analytical in nature and uses deductive reasoning to determine who other people are, what they think, and how they perceive their environment. This ego operates as a defense mechanism for the self image. It is susceptible to the mental poison of hatred, which can manifest as hatred for others or self hatred for not living up to an idealized self. Hatred is further transformed into one of three poisons. The first is envy, which develops into Ego-Flattery also known as Over Independent, the second is hatred itself, which develops into Ego-Go also known as Over Efficient, and the last is Jealousy, developing into Ego-Melancholy also known as Over Reasoner.

Adaptation Instinct

The Adaptation Instinct is attached to the nervous system. This instinct controls thoughts, actions and work. It functions as the intellectual center searching to acquire and apply knowledge. This instinct interprets large ideological principles and societal constructs. The Practical Ego comes from this instinct. This ego wants to finish tasks and get things done, but it often cannot do this because it is in constant conflict with the other two instincts. The Practical Ego constantly asks the question "Where am I?", seeking knowledge required to adapt and survive in the environment. It uses Empathetic reasoning to construct hypothetical scenarios to determine what we could do if we were placed in certain situations so that we may prepare ourselves for those possibilities if they become reality. This ego develops into the mental poison of deceit, specifically self deceit in the form of delusions and anxiety attached to execution of ideas. As with the other mental poisons, deceit develops into one of three other mental poisons. The first is confusion, which turns into Ego-Stinginess also known as Over Observer; The second is deceit itself, which turns into Ego-Cowardice also known as Over Adventurer; and the third is mythomania (pathological lying), which turns into Ego-Planning also known as Over Idealist.

The Nine Fixations

Ichazo broke the instincts down into nine different fixations derived from the mental poisons discussed earlier; each with two different names. One name format is represented by Ego-X, and other is represented as Over-X. For example, enneagram type 1 is referred to as both Ego Resentment and Over Perfectionist. Descriptions of the types can also differ depending on which attributes are emphasized and are more evident in certain types such as type 2, which we will discuss further in a later section. Ichazo proposed that we move through each of the nine fixations during our lives, but we tend toward one point most often, that which we call home.

1-Ego-Resentment/Over-Perfectionist

The first point on the enneagram of fixations, which correlates to modern enneagram type 1 is known as Ego-Resentment or the Over-Perfectionist. This fixation is hyper critical of everything it views as less than perfect. Criticism from this fixation is applied to both external and internal events of the self and others. It is trapped by perfection, nothing worldly will ever be perfect, but it will criticize without end until perfection is reached. Of course, this results in the person becoming perpetually critical, which is why it is described as a trap. Each fixation is ruled by a certain passion. The passion attached to this fixation is anger, which is appropriate since it is the result of a resentful and critical world view. In order to break free from this fixation, the individual must learn to accept that the universe is nothing but perfect because the universe is in constant flux and the components therein are ever changing to fit the physical laws of the universe; or in another sense, everything in the universe is already perfect and that everything must be perfectly built to adhere to the great laws of the universe.

2-Ego-Flattery/Over-Independent

This fixation is a little more ambiguous than the last. According to Ichazo's students when recalling his teachings, Ego-Flattery is a fixation of pride, one that needs approval from others. It engages in flattery constantly so that it may receive flattery as well. It wants freedom but traps itself with dependence on attention and approval from others. For an individual to break free from this fixation the person must learn to be free from dependence on outside approval and learn to live in a humble way.

Ichazo gives a slightly different explanation in his book, *The Human Process for Enlightenment and Freedom*. Notice the students were describing Ego-Flattery whereas Ichazo is describing the Over Independent.

They are the same fixation, but different aspects are accentuated in each description.

> The same thing happens in the over independent. Outside he acts independently, making his own decisions. Though, when he turns inside, he finds chaos. In a frantic effort to control his own world, he is going to destroy his independent act. He is so preoccupied with his independence that he never has it.

At first glance, congruence of Ego Flattery and Over Independent seems questionable. However, we can realign the two if we consider the approval seeking nature of Ego Flattery and the rebellious need for control of the Over Independent to both be acts of pridefulness, each representing a side of the same coin. Naturally, a person who is confident in their own abilities will not need to depend on anyone. The Over Independent becomes so preoccupied with their independence that they turn to outside approval for assurance. Thus, losing independence entirely. This is the same trap mentioned in the descriptions of Ego-Flattery and bridges the gap between the two descriptions.

3-Ego-Go/Over-Efficient

This fixation is at the center of the Living Group (The Living Group is another term for the feeling or heart triad) and believes that the universe itself depends on their individual efficiency. Therefore, this individual works himself and those close to him to death attempting to become increasingly more efficient. Though 100% efficiency is impossible to reach, this individual will nevertheless strive for it, thus creating his own trap. He attempts to cover up problems by outworking them, solving conflict created by his need for efficiency with ever more efficient maneuvers, fooling those around him into believing he is fine. In reality, he is increasingly less happy, simply acting as he believes he should to keep those around him happy. To remedy this fixation, he must take a step back from work, taking time to realize that the universe is just as efficient as ever without his constant efforts. This will allow him to find peace, knowing that the world will not stop if his efficiency falters.

4-Ego-Melancholy/Over-Reasoner

Once again, Ichazo's students produced a slightly different description from what Ichazo published. John C. Lilly interpreted Ego Melancholy as a fixation of perceived suffering and sadness. This individual views other people's lives as much happier than their own, causing him to envy his neighbor's good fortune, and fall into the perpetual trap of hoping that his happiness is just around the corner. Just as with the Over Independent, let's look at Ichazo's slightly different interpretation of this fixation in *The Human Process for Enlightenment and Freedom*.

> The over-reasoner wants to understand the outside and to find beautiful reasons. But he over-reasons and never finds those beautiful reasons. He is always going to have a question because he doesn't have explanations for the reasons. When turning inside, the over reasoner will reason about himself, and will continue asking "why?" and "why?" indefinitely. Whatever the reason is, there is always going to be another "why?"

Ichazo gives further clarity to this description in his letter to the Arica School.[3]

> The Reasoner questions "why," not in a transcendental way, but in a small, personal way as in, "why was I born a woman," "why are my parents such and such?"

"Why doesn't anybody love me?" If they go out shopping on a rainy day, they will ask, "Why does it have to rain when I go shopping?" The constant questioning exhibited by the Reasoner is that of a person taking too much of the weight of the world on their shoulders. Because of this, they are extremely susceptible, believing they are constantly cheated, and they see the world in general as being opposed to them, not giving them their "fair share."

This description shows us how Lily's interpretation of the Over Reasoner's envious and sad nature aligns with Ichazo's representation. Individuals can break free of this fixation by realizing that everyone's existence is governed by the same universal laws. In doing so, they will come to know they have not been singled out to suffer; instead, they will realize we are all equal.

5-Ego-Stinginess/Over-Observer
Ego-Stinginess keeps the contents of the mind private because of constant feelings of inadequacy. It isolates itself from the world, becoming a perpetual observer. This individual is greatly intrigued by life, watching from the outside looking in, but never engaging in life itself. Observation traps this fixation, forever

attempting to see things from all sides while hiding from the world in fear of exposing his perceived inadequacy. This behavior is a product of the passion of avarice, or greed. Greed here refers to the fixation's tendency to withhold thoughts, never fully divulging the inner workings of his mind, so that he may exist in a constant cycle of observation. This fixation never wants to fully expose itself because it does not trust the outside world, nor its own capabilities to handle obstacles in the world. To break free, this individual must stop hiding in his own mind and experience all life has to offer. He needs to escape his own mind and stop holding back so that he may embrace the world, and fully participate in life.

6-Ego-Cowardice/Over-Adventurer

Ego-Cowardice, as one can guess, is driven by fear. As the center of the Doing Group (another term for the thought or mind triad), it seeks to accomplish things, but it is frozen by fear and therefore is incapable of accomplishing anything at all. This fixation is riddled with anxiety, seeing danger everywhere, even where danger does not exist. Thus, this individual seeks safety from this perceived danger, often finding security in a strong leader, religion, or ideology. This fixation is trapped by the need for security. Once Ego-Cowardice finds the security it craves, it will begin to find flaws in its secure position, perceiving or even imagining more and more potential threats. The passion of this fixation is fear. Ego-Cowardice finds threats everywhere and, therefore, fears the world, constantly worried that his efforts and the efforts of those around him will end in disaster. This individual seeks great adventures and understanding but limits himself with his own fear. To break free of this fixation, the individual must find the courage to face the world and acknowledge that remaining stagnant is more harmful to his spirit than calculated risks.

7-Ego-Planning/Over-Idealist

Ego-Planning, as the name implies, comes up with grandiose and elaborate plans of how to improve the world. This fixation is idealistic in nature, fully believing in the plans it makes. The plans, however, are never realistic. They are optimistic and always impractical. Thus, this fixation is trapped by its own idealism, constantly scheming, and carrying out its plans with great enthusiasm, only for the plans to fail because they are not based in reality. The passion of this fixation is gluttony. Gluttony in the form of unending and increasingly idealistic plans despite failing time and time again. The individual can break out of this fixation by learning to embrace the present and fully live in the moment, instead of dreaming of a perfect future.

8-Ego-Vengeance/Over-Justice-Maker

Ego-Vengeance is hypersensitive to anything he perceives as injustice. This individual responds to injustice by seeking revenge, often resulting in physical damage to the transgressor or the transgressor's environment. This fixation is always in pursuit of perfect justice and rebels against the outside world until justice is upheld. This pursuit of unattainable justice is the trap of Ego-Vengeance. Similar to the plight of Ego-Resentment, this fixation is searching for a form of perfection that will never be reached, thus it becomes angry and lashes out at the world. Anger is the passion of this fixation, often manifesting in excessive forms of retaliation in response to perceived injustice. This individual's response to injustice is often so extreme that physical harm is done to both the transgressor and the host of the fixation. It destroys imperfect examples of justice in search of a non-existent perfect form and thus continues to destroy indefinitely.

This individual must learn to approach situations with no expectation of justice in order to break free from his fixation. He must learn to live without the constraints of justice entirely.

9-Ego-Indolence/Over-Non-Conformist

Ego-Indolence is situated at the top of the enneagram and is an especially unique fixation. Unique because we all possess this fixation to a certain extent.[6] Ego-Indolence is the tendency to search for comfort and love through relationships with the environment and people around us rather than turning inward. This fixation sits at the center of the Being Group, also known as the gut or instinctive triad. It is constantly searching for how it ought to be, always turning to outside cues and never being itself. The fixation falls for the trap of seeking, looking on the outside for what can only be found within. Seeking gives way to the passion of laziness because this individual never takes responsibility for cultivating his own mind, instead he sticks to comfortable routines The individual must realize that each individual is deserving of love in order to break free from this fixation. This lack of unconditional or holy love is an innate characteristic of humanity created by our tendency to be stuck in routines and neglect cultivation of our own personalities and minds. [2] [4] [5]

Sources:

https://wiki.personality-database.com/link/21#bkmrk-oscar-ichazo%27s-lette

[1] Oscar Ichazo's Letter to the Transpersonal Community - Letter_to_the_Transpersonal_Community_1991_by_Oscar_Ichazo.pdf

[2] The Human Process for Enlightenment and Freedom - https://de.catbox.moe/vf464i.pdf

[3] The Ultimate Purpose of the Arica School - https://de.catbox.moe/53m4h9.pdf

[4] The Arica Training according to John C Lilly and Joseph E Tart - The_Arica_Training_by_John_C._Lilly__Joseph_E._Hart_Transpersonal_Psychologies_1975_2.pdf

[5] Arica Week 6 - 7 according to Winifred Rosen - http://www.icwa.org/wp-content/uploads/2015/11/WR-6.pdf

[6] Interviews with Óscar Ichazo - https://de.catbox.moe/udf8ru.pdf

The Enneagram of Personality

The language and approach of Ichazo was one of a philosopher and sage. It was Claudio Naranjo who would place modern psychological terms and a scientific approach on the Enneagram.

Claudio Benjamín Naranjo Cohen (24 November 1932 – 12 July 2019) was a Chilean-born psychiatrist. He is considered a pioneering force in the integration of psychotherapy and spiritual traditions. He was one of the three successors named by Fritz Perls (founder of Gestalt Therapy), and a founder of the Seekers After Truth Institute. Naranjo learned of Oscar Ichazo's enneagrams while attending a training retreat with others from the United States in Arica, Chile sometime around 1970. Though the enneagram was only a small part of the material Ichazo presented. Later in 1971, Ichazo introduced his works on the enneagram to the United States through the Arica Institute. Naranjo incorporated the enneagram into his own teachings and developed the enneagram along an entirely separate path from Ichazo.

For an outline of Naranjo's ideas and contributions, we can look to the Naranjo Institute in the U.K. In the publication "Seekers After Truth" they write:

"The Enneagram of Personality" is a diagram of humanity reportedly deriving from diverse and ancient esoteric traditions. The name Enneagram derives from the Greek for nine (ennea) and refers to its formulation as nine points organized on the circumference of a circle. Each of the nine points refers to a personality or character type, and collectively they form a comprehensive depiction of human 'error', virtue, and potential.

Each of nine types is associated with a particular set of emotional, cognitive and behavioral inclinations or compulsions that together form a basic worldview and modus operandi. At the core of this edifice is a reliance on a particular emotional drive. Radiating from this core emotion is a corresponding cognitive inclination, a particular idea about the world. This serves both to shore up and to channel the underlying emotion. Though the Enneagram affords many complex permutations and nuances through a variety of considerations (such as Wings and Sub-types) this emotional and cognitive bias is the nucleus of each of the nine enneatypes.

According to Dr. Naranjo this emotion/cognition dyad can be summarized for each personality type by the following key words:

Anger – Perfectionism

Pride – False abundance

Vanity – Self-deception, Attractiveness

Envy – False lack

Avarice – Detachment

Fear – Accusation

Gluttony – Indulgence, Fraudulence

Lust – Vengeance, Intensity

Indolence – Self-forgetting

It is from the perspective of one of these emotion/cognition dyads that each individual will construct behavioral strategies to defend themselves against experience and reality. Whilst the emotional, cognitive and behavioral strategy is particular to each enneatype, broadly speaking they serve the same ends – to limit the experience or awareness of anxiety and suffering. Such avoidance is natural and inevitable, a necessary survival mechanism in our negotiation of our relationship to ourselves and to the world. We are all obliged by nature and by circumstance to construct an identity, a strategy for presenting ourselves to the world.

Whilst enabling on the one hand, on the other hand this same personality is limiting to the degree that its construction requires the systematic negation of elements of ourselves or the world that do not conform to its mold. To be in personality is therefore to be out of contact with a more comprehensive view of the world. To be in personality is to be wearing blinders, or blue or red or green tinted spectacles such that we see the world (including ourselves) as red or green or blue. It is to be on "automatic" plot, slightly roboticized, and no longer free to respond to the world and reality from an uninhibited emotional, cognitive or behavioral palette, from the free flow of instinct. To be in personality is to have lost the spontaneity of the infant, and the contact with self of the newly born.

The therapeutic function of the Enneagram of Personality is to identify the precise form of rigidity that we have constructed for ourselves in place of spontaneity and 'being'. Which suit of armor did we don at a certain point in our history, and subsequently confuse for our skin? Which mask did we confuse with our real face? To discover this armor or mask permits a degree of distinction between our sense of personality and our sense of self. By allowing this distance we can begin to understand that we are more than we appear to be, that our personality is not just the way we reveal ourselves in and to the world, it is the way we have hidden or lost contact with much of what we think and feel, and with the free flow of our instincts. We can begin to wonder what it might be like 'to be' outside, or beyond personality, and to shed light on that within us that has remained in personality's shadow. In theory, once we realize that our personality is a manipulation of ourselves and the world, involving a degradation in our ability to perceive and operate fully within reality, we can begin to examine and reveal to ourselves new ways of thinking, feeling, and doing.

To this end the Enneagram of Personality offers us antidotes - attitudes and values that we can cultivate that will help to loosen, in time, the grip of our passions and cognitive fixations that constitute our "automatic" and defended self. Likewise, as a diagrammatic system, the Enneagram permits us to locate other ways of being in the world and our relationship to these 'others'. Thus, the Enneagram provides us not only with a diagnosis of our malady, but also with very loose prescriptions, clues, pointers, and avenues to explore how we might become more than we apparently are, 'other' than what we are, or re-discover our capacity for spontaneity, understood as a non-automatic, healthy, and organismic response to reality.

It is on this shifting crossroads between malady and cure, neurosis and virtue, that the long journey of the work on self occurs."
(This ends the quote from Seekers After Truth.)

Naranjo's Enneatypes

According to enneagranusedguide.com, Naranjo called his version of the Enneagram types "enneatypes" and described them in terms of a trait structure (what follows can be found in his books Ennea-type Structures and Character and Neurosis).

1-Angry Virtue -
Anger and Perfectionism
Anger, Criticality, Demandingness, Dominance, Perfectionism, Over-Control, Self-Criticism Discipline.

2-Egocentric Generosity -
Pride, Love, Need, Hedonism, Seductiveness, Assertiveness, Nurturance and False Abundance, Histrionism, Impressionable Emotionality.

3-Success Through Appearances-
Vanity, Inauthenticity, and the "Marketing Orientation"
Attention Need and Vanity, Achieving Orientation, Social Sophistication and Skill, Cultivation of Sexual Attractiveness, Deceit and Image Manipulation, Other-

Directedness, Pragmatism, Active Vigilance, Superficiality

4-Seeking Happiness through Pain -

Envy and the Masochistic Personality

Envy, Poor Self-Image, Focus on Suffering, "Moving Toward", Nurturance, Emotionality, Competitive Arrogance, Refinement, Artistic Interests, Strong Superego

5-Seeking Wholeness through Isolation -

Avarice and Pathological Detachment

Retentiveness, Not Giving, Pathological Detachment, Fear of Engulfment, Autonomy, Feelinglessness, Postponement of Action, Cognitive Orientation, Sense of Emptiness, Guilt, High Superego, Negativism, Hypersensitivity

6-The Persecuted Persecutor -

Fear and Suspiciousness

Fear, Cowardice and Anxiety, Over-Alert Hyper intentionality, Theoretical Orientation, Ingratiating Friendliness, Rigidity, Pugnacity, Orientation to Authority and Ideals, Accusation of Self and Others, Doubt and Ambivalence

7-Opportunistic Idealism -

Gluttony, Fraudulence, and Narcissism

Gluttony, Hedonistic Permissiveness, Rebelliousness, Lack of Discipline, Imaginary Wish, Fulfillment, Seductive Pleasingness, Narcissism, Persuasiveness, Fraudulence

8-Coming on Strong -

Lust and Vindictive Arrogance

Lust, Punitiveness, Rebelliousness, Dominance, Insensitivity, Conning and Cynicism, Exhibitionism (Narcissism), Autonomy, Sensorimotor Dominance

9-Going with the Stream –

Accidia (Sloth), the Passion for Comfort and the Overadjusted Disposition

Psychological Inertia, Over-Adaptation, Resignation, Generosity, Ordinariness, Robotic Habit-Boundedness, Distractibility.

Coming after Naranjo, there were individuals who structured and propagated the theories of the Enneagram. They wrote books, spread knowledge, and taught classes. Some added tests in the form of questions or multiple-choice selections in order to help the reader or student more accurately determine which type they are. Don Riso, Russ Hudson, and Helen Palmer are but a few of these.

A Comparison of Numerology and the Enneagram

Enneagram Types and How They Compare to Numerology

Source materials used in this comparison, along with other research are provided by permission of and collaboration with the following authors.

Enneagram: Finding Your Type and Making Sense of the System by Breandan Lumpkin, published by Fifth Estate, Inc. 2022 ISBN 979-8369874578

Numerology, A Book of Insights by Anne Burton, published by Fifth Estate, Inc. 2007 ISBN: 9781933580456

Author's Note: It is my fondest hope that by contrasting and comparing the vast resources of knowledge, both old and new, that fresh insights may be gained in the field of study within the Enneagram community. The information is here, it simply has to be approached with an open mind and fresh sight.

Enneagram 1s:

Desires to be good, correct, accurate, right

Fears being wrong, incorrect, or unacceptable. Fears being viewed as bad or unethical

High standard for their work and performance

Imposing standards on others

Serious and straightforward

Rude and unyielding

Principled and lives with strong moral values

Judgmental and critical

Rigid, stubborn, and resistant to change

Trailblazer, teacher, guide, inventor

Focused and attentive

Obsessive about the project at hand

Follows rules and regulations

Uses internal standards which are unexplained and unknown by others

Fears being imperfect

Judges others for being imperfect

Represses anger and frustrations

Vents anger by talking over people, arguing them down, and being overly critical

Numerology 1

1 is the type of the leader/reformer. They want to be right, to strive to improve others, to justify their position, and to be beyond criticism so as not ever to face condemnation. The ego looks strong but has been damaged in childhood. They aim for the ideal, not content to be as they are. They keenly feel the struggle between good and evil, head and heart, irrationality and their own rational minds. They are sure of themselves, (less because they are perfect and more because they are sure of their ideals). They see themselves as less than the ideals for which they strive. They subordinate themselves to an abstract ideal such as truth or justice. They embrace a work-oriented theology and ethic, thinking that one must work and strive toward an ideal. They may seem confused and disbelieving when they see that effort and hard work sometimes don't pay off. Whether it is because of fate or personal failure, 1's don't consider it fair when a return for

effort isn't forthcoming. They feel uplifted and set apart from the norm by this striving.

So as not to be condemned, they act as if they are perfect and right. They constantly measure the distance between themselves and the ideal, and also how far they have come. They are caught between having these ideals, and implementing them in the world. They repress many emotions and impulses, riding herd over them to keep them in check and live up to their idealistic aims. Despite their apparent strength of will and character, this repression and striving (which may be to seek the father image's approval) can cause obsessive/compulsive behavior.

They desire to be liked and accepted. They get very lonely at times inside of their self-sufficient facade. 1's are the extroverted thinking type. They elevate objective reality and formula to the ruling principle for themselves and their environment. By this criteria all abstracts are measured (good, evil; beauty, ugliness).

Everything that agrees with the formula is right, and the rest is wrong. People must also conform to it. All who don't are immoral, wrong, and going against the universal laws. As we can see, if this law is broad enough it may serve a sociological purpose; however, it seldom is and provides nothing more than a whipping post by which he forces himself and others into his mold. They will get angry at others when they are really angry at themselves for not being perfect.

The superior function of 1 is mental or thinking, the inferior function is emotional or feeling. In childhood the 1 identified negatively with the father image. The father may have been critical. In some way the child got the message that they were not acceptable as they were. They tried to become blameless by shifting blame, avoiding blame, and trying to be perfect. The message of "you must be better" drove them to repress many emotions and impulses.

They probably had help from a parent who punished them if they let an impulse slip or told them that they were bad, wrong, or unacceptable. He had few kind words for them. The father could have been stern, abusive, missing, critical, cold, or an alcoholic. The child was forced to be an adult and not to do or say anything wrong for fear of being punished. The child was not able to be a child, especially in the sense of the needed emotional freedom. They may have been called on to help raise younger siblings or keep the household running in some way. This can truncate a childhood and stop growth. At first they did not rebel;

instead they felt guilty for not performing up to some expected level and they felt frustrated.

The feeling of failure for not being good enough and the pressure of the critical environment begat anger, both at the parent and themselves. They tried to internalize the anger. The anger increases when they see that others do not have to conform to the same perfection that was laid upon them. The super-ego of the 1 now is imprinted with the values and critical inner voice of the parent. The voice that we all have that talks to us, critiques us, encourages us, and gives us that running commentary comes partly from the super-ego. It is our internal parent. They push themselves toward perfection, just as they felt in their childhood. At its worst, they repress their wants and desires in exchange for doing only what is right and correct in order to silence the inner voice.

Isn't it odd that from the time we are old enough to identify with those in authority over us to the time that we die, we strive to please them, or rebel against them? This is the choice that the 1 type will make. They will either be hard, egocentric, willful, and defiant; or they will be perfectionists, driving themselves to the point of exhaustion, probably remembering words from their past such as, "you are lazy", or "you are stupid."

They don't understand that others are not as driven as they are. They usually don't really understand what drives them until they are stopped by some situation that forces them to take time enough to look inside. They can come to resent those who can do as they wish without the interference of an inner voice. As the 1 goes to the limits they may forsake trying to quiet the voice, and rebel against all social rules. They may even form a kind of split in which they perform as adults when around those that they know, and as a child at other times.

The child within them is forced into a defensive attitude due to the discomfort of being wrong "all of the time", (even though by now the majority of the insufficiency that they feel is from themselves), so they have a hard time admitting that they are wrong. They become opinionated and loud so as not to be challenged. They become critical of others as a defense against being criticized. At this point, they usually show signs of stress and nervousness, having repressed much anger and fear from their past. The aim is to silence the critic within, so they may turn to excesses of drink, drugs, or sex. They may have crying spells or spells of rage that temporarily reduce the pressures.

The 1 has to realize that their way is familiar to them, but it is not the only way. Others have different stresses driving them. There is more than one right way. They also need to see that when they were young, love was a reward for being good, but that is not the way that it should be. True love asks for nothing but its own expression. They must break with the old ways and old voices within and come to accept themselves and others without fear of rejection.

We are all imperfect, yet we all should be loved. We have to forgive all of the cuts, criticisms, and demands placed on us in the past and to allow ourselves to be less than perfect. We should see ourselves as the people that we are, better than some, worse than some, just a person who is trying, and if we could be satisfied with that, we could feel a release from our self-imposed prison.

1's deepest need is to feel that they are loved even though they are imperfect. The sad thing is, they can't love themselves due to the inner voice of their parents judging them all of the time. This view of the 1 allows us to see a vulnerable, needy side of the 1 type. The child within has braced his small frame against the next cut and waits with defiant tears for the one who will accept him as he is. The defiance is what shows, not the child. They are very concerned with how others view them, although they may not admit it. They judge situations against a view of potential perfection (how perfect it could be versus how far it falls short). Those are old ways that did not serve them well. They must seek a release from them now.

Healthy 1's are wise, discerning, and tolerant. Realistic and balanced in judgment. These 1's are rational, moderate, principled, objective, and ethical. High integrity, a teacher, leader. They try not to let their feelings get in the way of good judgment. They allow their emotions to surface, and they discover that they are not as chaotic as they had been led to believe. They lay aside the rules to try simply to become complete people. They have a moral vision and are sought for guidance. They can understand and tolerate different points of view without having to agree or enforce them. They are passionate about righteousness and justice. They live their convictions, even if it means going against civil law. Their goodness is a deep satisfaction to them. At their best they are original, creative, progressive, determined, optimistic, willpower, leader, individualistic, direct, to the point, self-starters, courageous, pioneering.

Average 1's are high-minded idealists, striving for excellence. The reformer, crusader, and advocate. These 1's are orderly, efficient, and impersonal. They are too emotionally controlled; they can also be critical, judgmental, opinionated, perfectionists, and moralizing. Indignant, angry, abrasive. They can exhort themselves and others to improve. They find it hard to allow others their views. They have an elitist, noble, lofty sense of self. They take on the challenge of righting moral and social wrongs, educating and guiding others. This is because they do not trust anyone else to do it correctly. They have classified almost everything as right or wrong, and expect others to do as they are told. They have the zeal of a missionary. They are articulate and love to debate points of view. They want the rational mind to rule everything. Meticulous, precise, sticklers. Life is serious business. They cannot delegate work.

The unhealthy 1 can be very self-righteous, intolerant, dogmatic, and inflexible. They cannot stand to be wrong. They tend to preach one thing and do as they please. They can be cruel and punitive to others.

Obsessive/compulsive behavior or sudden nervous breakdown and depression are possible. They think in error that they have attained the unattainable ideal for which they strove. They think that they alone can do the job or have the truth. They are argumentative. They view people as malleable to their will. Nothing is ever good enough. "I'm not having fun, so neither will you." They are dogmatic. They are so aware of their thoughts and impulses that they can become obsessed because of impulsive thoughts of sex, heresy, or violence, that they may even think that it is demonic. This is also a way of shifting blame. They have no mercy, love, or sympathy. When others don't act according to the 1's moral code they can have them burned at the stake. In their fear of being condemned, they will quickly and mercilessly condemn others. Unhealthy 1's can be described as selfish, egocentric, aggressive, arrogant, bullish, bossy, proud, and unable to admit mistakes.

1's will act out by setting very high standards and obsessing about not living up to them, and by rationalizing their way out of admitting their shortcomings. They have feelings of bitterness and disappointment at having fallen short of some mark. These feelings are often blamed on others, or the world in general. They become angry, impatient, and rude. They judge others and feel "put upon." They become rebellious and tyrannical, leaving no room for any opinion but their own. They won't listen to reason. They think that everything is imperfect, and it's their job to tell others the best way to set things right.

All of their angst of what they are feeling about themselves is projected into others. They feel imperfect yet driven to be perfect. Anger and despair can be the only result. The 1 needs to let go of unreasonable standards, the fear of losing control, being blind to their own inconsistent thoughts and ways, disappointment with themselves and the world, driving themselves and others too hard, and being easily annoyed. The 1 should focus on his ability to be independent, self-motivated, creative, pioneering, capable, and a leader.

1's will work out their problems by reminding themselves that it is all right not to be perfect…that others count just as much as they do. 1's must learn to differentiate between the rights and lives of others and themselves. Relax and trust others to do things their own way in their own lives. It will take much of the pressure off. Slow down and be softer, more compassionate, and more concerned for others. Enjoy life more. Understand that the feelings that you have about your self-image is not fact. It is the echo of long past voices of those who had their own ego problems.

We must all learn that feelings are not facts. They only become facts when they line up with reality. If you stop right now and make a checklist of what most people consider normal and correct, you will find that you fall well within the limits of being an exacting person. This being fact, now you must work on adjusting your feelings accordingly. In a nut shell, be less critical of all, and that includes yourself.

Enneagram 2s:

Desires to be wanted, loved, needed as a companion, appreciated

Fears being unloved, unwanted, not appreciated, becoming too needy

Helpful and inviting

Can be too trusting

Meaningful relations and connections are their first choice

They are selfless, devoted friends

They can be taken advantage of

Twos are great partners in life and business

They can impose themselves into situations to help, even when not wanted or invited

Can commit more than what is needed

They are generous, empathetic, and compassionate, sometimes to the point of losing themselves in others

Find joy in connecting with family and friends

Numerology 2

2s want to be loved, to express their feelings for others, to be needed and appreciated. They will coerce and manipulate others using guilt or passive-aggressive acts to get their emotions out and keep others where they want them. They also need others to need and want their love; they need to think that they are emotionally correct and will hide their true motivations from others and themselves. Healthy 2s make wonderful mates. They are capable of sensing and serving the needs of their mates, at times, even before they verbalize them. They are individuals yet are able to be very empathetic.

If 2's are not healthy they will have strong feelings that tend to be over-expressed. The positive will be stressed and the negative side will be ignored. This leads to obsessions and self-deception. They may be blind to their own aggressive feelings making them manipulative, passive/aggressive, and selfish in the name of love.

The negative 2 is the most insidious of personality types. Their love is not free but many times has strings attached. This is because the parent communicated his love in a conditional way, the parent withheld approval and affection if the child disappointed them, or they did not approve of the child's actions or decisions. The child grew up expecting this and thinking that it was correct. Yet they feel hurt and angry and are ill-equipped to reason out why. They grow up on the emotional edge of love and anger.

They are an extroverted feeling type. Often only a small change in situations is needed to cause a large emotional shift. This is because of an unacknowledged anger present just below the surface. There was an ambivalence to the father or father image. This sets the stage for ambivalence toward those who can give them love. This problem of relating to the father makes their love conditional. They seem to think that they must be absolutely good to deserve love, even to love themselves. This may explain why they must ignore the bad in themselves and others. It can get bad enough that they will defend their manipulation in the name of love, even against the facts. Religion plays an important part in the life of 2s'. It gives them a value system that they can relate to, with which to verbalize their emotions.

The opposite is that they are busybodies, and meddlers, not knowing the difference between what is good and what is God. They wear themselves out being good, and can be heard to say, "I believe God told me to do this." We must be very careful not to use phrases like that lightly. It leaves others in a position of not being able to help them for fear of having it said that they are fighting against someone who is following a higher lead. 2s must also be aware that since the super-ego is the internalized parent, and God is the ultimate parental image, we can easily confuse the echoes of what our internal parent is saying and the leading of our higher power.

It is easier to see the 2 in catch phrases such as "I'm just trying to make things easier for you," or "I'm doing this for you." They usually have ulterior motives. Most of the time we all have an aim for doing good deeds and we should acknowledge it, at least to ourselves. Honesty to ourselves is the most important thing. If we were totally honest about our actions and goals we would find that the early church fathers were correct when they said that every action and thought of man stems from some form of selfishness. The 2s won't acknowledge this in themselves but will remind you of your problems and prick at your heart's wounds while saying that they'll be there for you because you need them. They are always trying to create the need so that they can fill it.

2s need to be needed. 2s often feel a pull between heart and head. If it gets too bad there are obsessions, hypochondria, headaches, migraines, or stomach problems. As a last word we should "love and do what you will," and not let the word love be a license to do what we want.

The superior function of a 2 is emotional or feeling, the inferior function is mental or thinking. 2s need to feel loved and important in the lives of others. As children, they felt as though they had to earn the affection of the parent through service, compliance, and by being careful not to go contrary to the emotions of the parent. They may flatter and serve in order to "buy" a person's love. They need approval. This may be a transference from the fact that they worked so hard for a parent's approval. They then tend to transfer that action over to others that they love.

2s will try to become what others need. They will say what others want to hear. This suppresses their real personality, as well as spawning insecurity about being "found out" not to be real. This may drive them deeper to the point of losing their identity to their partner's will. They trade this for security and protection that is associated with the partner, who has usually been chosen for their strong will and personality. They believe that they know the innermost feelings of others, and they strive to serve and anticipate the needs based on that feeling.

The 2 is the most subservient of numbers. Those in the subservient role have to develop a sensitive empathy or a feeling of being almost telepathic at times in order to better fulfill the role of helper. The mature 2 is a model of the caring, sensitive person who is still an individual. It isn't until the 2 is mature that they realize that what they want out of the relationship is what they are putting into it. They will swing in their personality traits from extreme to extreme. Saint to whore, happy to angry, as they try to find a balance in themselves. It reveals situations where love was used as a tool, a reward system. Love, respect, and approval were used as a carrot in front of the child's nose to motivate them.

When unresolved anger is the driving force, there is always going to be pain inflicted. It can come with a gift, such as a comment like, "Here is a gift for you. Boy, did it cost, and I'm excited at having to go through so much to get it." This give and hurt or give and take is very common with 2s until the anger is dealt with. The catch is that since open anger is equated with doing better in school, being a good child, or performing better, they continue this in adult life by trying to anticipate their mate's wants and desires in order to be a good little boy or girl and to get the love that they need. As they grow more insecure, they will stoop to flattery, manipulation, and passive/aggressive pressure to get the mate to feel as if they owe the 2 something.

Rejection from the 2s point of view is the worst possible outcome and is to be avoided at all times. Even the feeling of this is repressed in the 2, so you may hear things such as "I'm not angry. I've forgiven the son of a bitch." 2s can serve so intently that they lose part of their identity. They put their needs on the shelf in order not to disappoint, and therefore lose connection with their loved ones. This yields the insecurity of being found out, and the stress of suppressing part of themselves. Thoughts and statements such as, "They wouldn't like me if they really knew me," can be common for the insecure 2. Even if they flirt outrageously, they usually just seek attention, to feel wanted or needed.

2s watch for clues to see what people want or like, so they may be the provider of it and earn a place in the life of the lover or friend. They are true givers. In the romantic phase of a relationship the 2 is totally committed to serving and fitting themselves to the mate, but as pressure starts to build there can be emotional, hysterical, or angry outbursts which may seem unprovoked or out of proportion to the stimuli. It is. It has only been "crow-barred" into activity by the present problem, and like a snowball headed downhill, it has little relevance to the people that started it.

Here is a test for any number to see if you are talking about the base issue that is bothering you.

1. Ask yourself if talking about the issue in a non-confrontational way is helping to dissipate the emotions.

2. Do you keep going around in circles so that in the same conversation the same issues come up over and over?

3. Does the argument get side-tracked? That is, does it branch into unrelated but volatile areas?

4. Are you having the same arguments many times, thinking it is taken care of, only to have it come back up again?

If the emotions peak instead of recede, if you find yourself back at the start with nothing accomplished, if you find yourselves arguing about many things, and if you continue to have the same fights after thinking it is resolved, you are probably not fighting about what is really at the base of the issue. 2s are good at hiding in the role of the victim, even though they may have created a hostile environment by reminding their mate about their mistakes and giving rise to their pain only to point out how good the 2 is because they have forgiven them and will help them be a better person.

Sounds good on the surface, doesn't it? When God said that he would forgive us, he said that he would throw our sins into the sea of forgetfulness and he would remember them no more. We must all strive to be more God-like. This doesn't mean that we should let someone hurt us over and over. God's prerequisite was that we were repentant, and a truly repentant person will strive not to make that mistake again. That is not a guarantee that they will be successful, only that they will try.

The 2 should follow this simple rule: if you can forgive a shortcoming, then forget it. If you can't forgive it, then tell the person openly that you can't, and that you will probably nag them about it. You could try a time of honest "in their face" anger, and vent what is really bothering you. I would be willing to bet that it will clear the air and healing will start. Just be sure that you know the real issue.

Healthy 2s are unselfish, altruistic, caring, empathetic, and helpful. They are capable of unconditional love. They understand that love is a gift. They find joy in giving. Able to love the sinner and forgive the sin. Philanthropic, uplifting, the good parent image. Looking out for others first, healthy emotional attachments, sympathetic, patient, diplomatic, receptive, considerate, maternal, sensitive to rhythm, detail-oriented, collects and assimilates information well. In Numerology, the healthy, integrated 2 is referred to as an eleven. These are the progressives, diplomats, and reformers. They are idealists, inspiring the people around them to higher levels.

Average 2s are emotional, demonstrative, friendly, overly personal, mothering, possessive, thinking their emotional input is more important than it is. 2s are somewhat histrionic. They have the ability to declare their feelings. They like physical and emotional contact. They can meet people and immediately regard them as friends. The average 2 talks about love and caring more than they act on it.

Unhealthy 2s are manipulative, using guilt or casting themselves as martyr, victim, or using hypochondria to get their way. They harbor feelings of anger, bitterness, and resentment, especially if others don't feel the way the 2 wants them to. When they do not feel loved it hurts the 2 and it calls into question their self-worth. They can prick at the soft spots of others with one hand and soothe them with the other. This passive-aggressive action confuses others. They can love and hate them at the same time. They will remind you of your shortcomings and bring you to self-doubts while telling you that they are good and forgiving enough to stay with you.

The unhealthy 2s are self-deceived and do not believe that they are anything but good and caring, even while they kill you with their kind of kindness. Fearful, dependent, overly sensitive, shy, petty, sullen, pouting, and apathetic; 2s may try so hard to please and appease that they make themselves into a slave.

2s will act out by emotional outbursts that may be triggered by a relatively small and unrelated issue, which is used as an excuse to vent their feelings regarding the real issue. They will point to the secondary issue as the cause of their rage and emotionally destructive behavior. The real problem is that they feel unappreciated, unloved, or unneeded. They are angry that they have not achieved the desired response from their efforts. They will attempt to manipulate or force the wanted feelings and reactions from the other person.

2s need to let go of feeling abused or taken advantage of, resentment, anger, hidden agendas, passive/aggressive behavior, trying to manipulate others into feeling or doing as they wish, fears of being alone or unloved, whining and complaining. 2s should focus on being a balanced, integrated part of a team effort, sensing what would help others, being a "helpmate," and their ability to be devoted, have patience, be precise, attend to detail, sensing rhythms and harmony in people.

2s will work it out by understanding their true feelings and why they feel them. They must then understand that no one has a right to manipulate the feelings of another. They must realize that just because others don't react in a particular way, it doesn't mean that they don't love you. The 2 must see that they are whole, complete, and lovable even if no one is "coupled" with them at the time.

Enneagram 3s:

Desires to be successful, admired, sought after, and seek name recognition

Fears being undervalued, not admired, a failure, unsuccessful

Will strive for success

They will avoid being thought of as ordinary

Their motivation is high

They need the admiration of others to feel affirmed and worthy

Because they are the actor, their inner world does not match their outside face or actions

They can deceive themselves in their roles and lose themselves

They are always cognizant of how people view them

They are socially conscious about their presentation

Because they are driven to succeed, leadership comes naturally

Success is paramount because it reflects on their image

Can present a refined, graceful style, expensive tastes, cars, clothes, and food

They have high expectations of themselves and their place in society

Numerology 3

3 wants to be affirmed. They thrive on attention, usually this is the limelight but it all centers around a feeling of being admired and accepted. They like impressing others with looks, talent, or ability. They can be status, style, and image-oriented. They are narcissistic. They interact with others well, but it is to defend against rejection which they fear. They are able to sense and respond to the emotions of others the way that plants respond to the sun - they turn toward the attention. They bask in it. They respond to the attention of others by imitating the values and ambiance of their psyche.

When the other people see themselves reflected favorably in the 3 they feel good about themselves and the 3. This establishes the "friendship" and the interaction is sustained. In childhood 3s identified closely with their mother image. They were given much attention when young. They were praised for performance, image, looks, or social skills. Because of this, they have a high and strong self-esteem. They expect others to accept and love them the same way their parental figures did. If they don't, this causes a feeling of rejection.

The 3 has an underdeveloped superego and an overdeveloped id and ego. This creates an arrogant air. They can manipulate and use others without remorse. At times if others don't admire them as the 3 thinks they should, they will strike out in anger, pouting, or vindictiveness as a child would. 3s need assurance and a way to feel like the spoiled child that they were with their mother image. 3s are performers, knowing what buttons to push to get people to like them. They seem sincere but are often empty. When the 3 turns to examine themselves, they get a balanced view of their self- worth and their abilities, acknowledging their faults and the equal worth of all, they will be modest, real, genuine, adaptable, and social people.

They strive to be the consummate type of the image that they have chosen. If they chose to be a yuppie, they will be the epitome of a yuppie. This is why there can appear to be a wide variety of kinds of 3s. They are activity and achievement driven. As children they could have been "Shirley Temple" types, as adults they may be socialites or workaholics, but they will perform in whatever they do. Like number 2 types, they can get lost in their own games. They can easily come to believe that they are the character that they play. If they dig deep enough, they will find that the role that they play is chosen to produce a certain kind of reaction from the "audience." They play for attention. As a child they were praised for achievements, as adults it is simply carried on.

It matters to them that a good image is presented - a perfect home, a perfect family, the storybook lover. They can even play the part of the sympathetic or suffering person, and not feel nearly as deeply as they can project. The first movement has to be to get in touch with their true feelings, with which they are very out of touch. Those they seem to have are the false stage that they often work from (a self-delusion). 3s were children who were asked how they did, not how they felt. They were rewarded for their performance. Image became more important than emotional connection. They learned to suspend their feelings in order to focus on getting attention and status. Being chameleon-like, they will adopt the image of the group. 3s can take it one step further. They are usually upbeat and optimistic. Their true identity becomes eclipsed by the game.

They tend to keep a surface optimism. Activity is an antidepressant for them. They are capable of doing and thinking of more than one thing at a time. If handled well and focused, this can be a great asset. If left unfocused, they can be scattered and "air-heads." 3s work toward material and financial acquisition in order to feel more secure about self.

In relationships 3s can put on the face of love. They may say and do what they think a lover should say and do without having the true feelings. They can easily deceive themselves. They try to fill as much time as they can with activity in order to keep inner emotions at bay. The actress or chameleon tendency is highest in the struggle to be accepted in their teenage years and young adulthood. They are competitive, with a type of competitiveness that lends itself to gossip, backstabbing, and being seen with only the right people.

3s are narcissistic in the fact that they are convinced that their way is right because they are superior and competent. This, however, is pride based on a false theme, not reality. Emotional intimacy is held at a distance due to the fact that they are afraid that the real self won't be loved. They, like the 2s, might say, "If they really know me they won't like me." But 3s have too much pride and an image to maintain, so they will continue until their ship sinks.

3s have a lot of energy and can think or do more than one thing at a time. In this, they resemble the 5. This can keep things lively, or can be a source of scattered energy where there is much activity and little accomplishment. The saddest thing about this number is that they fool people, and they know it. They are angered at the fact that people are fooled by their false face, yet they are afraid to show the real one in order that people love them. In a crisis, such as a mid-life crisis, a 3 may wake up to the fact that they were just playing a game, or aren't expressing the real them that has been bottled up for so long, at which time one should prepare for a change because they aren't the type to take it in stride. They will act.

3s should ask themselves, beyond the games and below the masks, "what is my true face? Until a 3 can look in the mirror and know in their heart who and what they are, they may easily and frequently fall victim to self-deception and the waste of time and pain it can bring for all involved. We all play games at one time or another. We all want to be something or someone else now and then, but we must keep in mind that it is only a game. Trying to make it permanent is a lie and is dangerous. 3... show your true face!!!

It will help the 3 immensely to know that most of us see through the exaggerations and games, and we have already accepted them in spite of the "crap." People would like them even more if they didn't have to wade through it. So, the fear that they have about falling short in people's eyes has already been realized, so they might as well relax and enjoy the unconditional love that they already have and don't know it. The superior function is emotional feeling, the inferior function is mental thinking.

Healthy 3s are inner directed, authentic, self-assured, energetic, adaptable, and ambitious. They like self-improvement. They can motivate others to be like them since they have many qualities to emulate. They are people in their potential state (in the process of making something out of themselves). They spend time making themselves better, more desirable, more attractive, smarter, and socially better. They are the all-American boy or girl - expressive, social, ambitious, conversational, inspirational, charming, gracious, artistic (through words, music, dance, sculpture, painting), and romantic.

Average 3s are concerned with prestige and status. Career and success are important. Image is top on their minds. They can be calculating manipulators, arrogant, pretentious, and narcissistic. They want to establish their superiority over others usually through competition. Being acknowledged by others as better raises their self-esteem. They compare job, salary, ability, and looks...as if to say, "Mine is better than yours." Because of this competitiveness, they may have trouble sustaining friendships. They have an egotistical air. They feel comfortable only around those they feel superior to. They are usually very successful since they pursue being the best with all their strength. They plot advancement relentlessly. Some have a "whatever it takes" approach. They are a marketing-oriented person (sell yourself). They seek to perfect their image instead of themselves. When an image is practiced long enough it takes on a false and empty life of its own.

Unhealthy 3s are exhibitionists. Sex, appearance, attraction, to influence others and get admiration. They may hold themselves away from others in a "look but don't touch" attitude. They get a kick out of frustrating others. They will do anything to "make it." Because of the child being spoiled or allowed to run wild, they have a superego shortfall, leading to a sociopathic treatment of others. They will use anyone that they need to.

A tip-off to this is the large number of relationships that they go through, none of which is long-term. They are sneaky, jealous, two-faced, and back-stabbing. Their battle cry is, "It isn't enough that I win, but others must fail." They enjoy lying, even if it is about nothing important. It gives them a rush. If the deterioration continues, sociopathy becomes psychopathy, and they could do anything. Since the problem stems from their mother, most acts will be against women. The unhealthy 3 is conceited, rude, a braggart, a liar, superficial, jealous, careless, a gossip, a flirt, a dilettante, shallow, and insincere.

3s act out through jealousy and revenge. They care so much about their image that they will do or say anything to establish and keep it. This includes exaggeration, verbosity, conspicuousness, and driving themselves too hard toward being the ideal of what they have chosen as an image. The image is not truly them; it is what they think others want to see. 3s need to let go of jealousy, envy, fear of rejection, fear of being humiliated or being inadequate. 3s must stop denying their feelings in order to fit in. Cease the thirst for admiration, need for constant attention, arrogance, driving too hard to be perfect, and the impulse to be fake. They need to focus on their ability to meet and interact with people; their flair for fashion, communications, or art; their persuasive personality, spontaneous creativity, and social sense.

3s will work out by trusting that the real self has more value than a fake self. If people like you when you are real they will like you for life. If they like the false you, they only like you as long as you are "playing." Realize that if you are secure in your own worth, you will not be threatened by the success of others.

Enneagram 4s:

Desires to stand out as unique and special, to find their place, to feel like they belong

Fears being insignificant, just another face in the crowd, common, unrecognized

Feels they are different from others

They are introspective as they seek ways to emote and express themselves

They are moody and can be unreliable when it comes to ordinary life

Their emotions and moods guide them so they may change perspectives often

Seek out those they believe understand them and they hate being lonely

Searches for a meaningful life and the meaning within life.

They seek respect and social recognition for their depth of feelings and expression

They are often disappointed when they discover that life does not care if they are special

In their dramatic life they attempt to find their real or ideal 'self', but they can lose themselves along the way

Feel that being melancholic and sad is part of the journey they are on

Numerology 4

4s want to understand themselves and to express this in some way that has beauty. They withdraw to attend to emotional needs or the pressure may overwhelm them. People who are represented by the number Four want to be unique. They are afraid of going unnoticed or unrecognized. They are craftsmen. They are natural-born engineers, scientists, and inventors of all kinds.

Fours want to revolutionize the world with new ideas and concepts. Many times they lack the tenacity, funds, or self-discipline to bring their new ideas to life, so they feel stuck, forgotten, rejected, and resentful. Generally, people hate new ideas that challenge their comfort zone, so there is always resistance to overcome. There are two motives for creative or artistic work; to communicate self, or to lose themselves in their work. There are two results from artistic or creative output: one is to transcend self, the other is to become self-aware.

If they choose to run from themselves the result will be delayed growth, lessened self-evaluation, lack of dependability, and escapism. It is only the healthy 4 that takes the high road. The average 4 instead turns inward to understand themselves. In doing so they become trapped in "subjectiveness." Entrapped in their emotions, or the urge to understand and control their emotions, they withdraw and have an increasingly difficult time coping with the world. They have emotional difficulties more than all other numbers. They sense both the full human potential and the depths to which we can descend; they view themselves as having missed their chance and potential and are destined to stagnate well below their station. The despair grows as they brood on what could have been or should have been.

The entire 4 process is driven by a search for identity. They want to sort out their emotions and answer the basic questions of "Who am I? " and "Is this all there is?". There is so much repression going on due to confusion or pain that they may not even be aware of their feelings until they are expressed through a medium. On first impressions they may seem shy or vulnerable, or you may see that they try too hard to fit in and that is their insecurity, but all of that fuels the inner conflict you'll see later. They will say "I'll live the way I want, and do things when I want", but that's an excuse to procrastinate because of uncertainty, or to be lazy, or irresponsible.

Most 4s lacked a role model. They didn't identify with either parent enough. There is a deep unconscious anger that one of the parents didn't nurture them. They are angry at themselves for being so defective that their parent left them. They could have had a feeling of aloneness in childhood, a piece missing by way of divorce, death, illness, alcoholism, or personality conflict with a parent. Usually, the father was the negative influence, so the child was forced to turn inward for their identity.

They feel that they were defective, and this caused the parent's lack of attention. They may try to be better, take up the slack for the parent, and make excuses for them, but in time they will begin to search themselves for the reason and turn within. They feel powerless and frustrated. This causes tension, self-doubt, and aggression. If the doubt or aggression is turned within, there will be compulsions, habits, and "isms" such as eating, drinking, drugs, or sex. These are the primary vehicles for escapism.

The ambivalence toward the parent can cause a rebellion in the child that is most clearly seen in the teens and twenties. They will defy authority, may even break the law, or drink to excess. They are acting out anger against a dysfunctional home. Some 4s come to believe their own lack of value. They tend to accept others for what they are without judging them.

Other 4s sink to a tough guy type of exterior, and even to a "thug." Mostly, 4s are needy people with a protective shell. They feel an isolation yet are trapped by a fear of intimacy brought on by a childhood feeling of not being worthy of stable loving closeness by both parents. The central cause of pain is an insidious type of emotional abandonment. The child always assumes that the parent is in the right and therefore they must be wrong. Their self-esteem plummets. They feel worthless and alone.

The despair that comes is partly due to the fact that they search for reasons as to why the parent doesn't love them when the problem is with the parent. They end up lost within themselves in despair trying to find a way to be good enough to make Daddy, or Mommy love them. This leads to despair, anger, and fatalism. They may dwell on the past, wondering where they went wrong, and lamenting what might have been. It is melancholia and is fought by outdoor activity and escapism.

Now and then, there is a loop that is formed in which the despair, (which is unresolved anger), leads to escapism in the form of drugs or alcohol. The escapism reinforces their own poor self-image of being worthless, which drives them deeper into despair. Even if drugs or drinking are not involved, they need to watch for such cycles of thought and habit. As blocked as the emotional Expression usually is, 4s can make the best artists, sculptors, chefs, or musicians. They seem to do it from the very core of their heart.

I want to encourage all of the 4s in the world to let go of their pain and view themselves as people of potential. Realize that no child is bad enough to warrant cruelty, neglect, or abandonment, so lay the blame where it belongs. Be angry, then get it out and go on with your life. Be expressive and open with your newly felt freedom. You have much to offer, not the least is an ability to put ideas into form. 4s want to have close, intense relationships but are self-conscious. Know you can overcome and be happy.

They may not be able to convey or demonstrate their love. Even saying "I love you" may be very uncomfortable for them. Their emotions are literally hog-tied, and remain that way until despair overtakes them, or they learn how to express feelings through a medium such as music or art.

Many 4s have a rough exterior. They may work in a tough, blue-collar job such as construction, trucking, farming, factory work or the like. This may be easier for them since no one expects a steel worker to open their heart and express their feelings (although no doubt there are exceptions). The superior function is physical sensing, the inferior function is intuitive.

Healthy 4s are inspired and creative. They are emotionally honest. Funny and serious. Emotionally strong. In touch with their inner impulses, and able to vent them creatively and without anger. They view both good and bad experiences as a growth process. They see all people as individuals and let them seek their own path without judgment. Disciplined, practical, orderly, methodical, industrious, conventional, honest, and reliable. They fit in well with social norms.

In Numerology the very healthy fours are referred to as 22s. They have broken free of that trap of depression and anger. Unlike the average 4 who has landed and settled where the winds of fate have swept them, the healthy 4 (22) is an enlightened, goal- oriented, ingenious, masterful individual. The apex of a 4 is represented in the person of Leonardo Da Vinci.

Average 4s can be into art or music, and trying to express their feelings through a medium. Sculpting, woodworking, gardening, or just manual labor to relax is included. They can become self-absorbed, moody, depressed, self-pitying, and indulgent. This gives way to decadence, impractical actions, escapism, and irresponsibility. Because this cycle is difficult to break, many 4s gravitate to blue-collar, mill work, construction, truck driving, and labor intensive jobs to keep down emotional or mental pressures.

Unhealthy 4s are emotionally blocked. Self-hatred, depression, hopelessness. In being unable to get in touch with their emotions, they don't love or accept themselves. They abuse drugs, drink, eating, sex, and even religion to escape. They do not exhibit social values and responsibility to society or others. These 4s are undisciplined, tend to procrastinate, show stubborn tendencies, have a limited viewpoint, become over-indulgent, crude, violent, vulgar, withdrawn, are unable to express their feelings. It is a dichotomy that on one side 4s are so attracted to beauty, art, self-expression, and feeling; and on the other hand they are introverted worriers whose emotions are blocked and repressed to the point of self-destructive behavior in the name of controlling themselves, their emotions, others, and the environment because of insecurity.

4s will act out by anger turned against themselves. This leads to hopelessness, despair, and self-destructiveness. Withdrawal from others through a tortured silence, drinking, drug abuse, overeating, and overindulgence are common in the worst cases.

4s need to let go of hurt feelings turned inward: escapism, self-destructiveness, hopelessness, despair, feeling inadequate, being shame driven, fatigue brought on by depression, dwelling on past mistakes or what could have been, laziness. They need to focus on their ability for logic, order, method, good memory, hard work, putting ideas into form and action, working with their hands, their ability to accept others for who they are, and down-to-earth common sense.

4s will work things out by getting an aim, or path in life, and starting to walk it. Get a direction and start making a difference in your life. You are lost in your feelings and aimlessness. Be gentle on yourself. Don't think that you have missed life, or that it is too late to change. Decide what you want to do, then go for it without self-condemnation. Don't judge yourself by your past, just do your best each day, and before you know it you will have accomplished your goals.

Enneagram 5s:

Desires to know, be informed, understand, capable, and look deeper into truths

Fears being blindsided due to lack of information or knowledge, incompetence, and ignorance

Deep thinkers

Quiet, shy, introverted

Lost in thoughts

Absent-minded

Lacks focus in daily life due to inner distractions

Aloof, walled off emotionally

Can be highly knowledgeable in certain areas

Think many times before speaking

Does not work well in large groups and prefers to work alone.

Mostly introverts

They hate small talk

They examine everything, and that includes long held ideas and beliefs

They do not care to maintain a status quo if it does not make sense or lacks proof

Between the systems of Enneagram and Numerology, types 5 and 7 are reversed. To keep the comparison of information between the systems synchronized, the numerology is reversed for the reader.

Numerology 7

7s are observers and can be very private people. Their world is a mental world. Even if they are not "mental giants," they tend to think and not to speak. Financial interaction is uncomfortable, obligations feel coercive, and relationships threaten their stance of emotional aloofness. Emotions are to be controlled. Intense competition is avoided. They remain in an aloof or self-protective posture. They are independent people who can be comfortable being alone for days at a time. Being an observer, they have a rather objective view of things.

They may seem emotionally cold or distant as they watch and observe people, or watch situations develop with an air of cool superiority, thinking that they'd never get involved in such foolishness. But the skeptical or cynical attitude that may develop is just a way of remaining emotionally removed. So is the mental snobbishness that some 7s have. The truth is they are uninvolved not because they are wiser, but because their fear of opening up and trusting is so low that it keeps them at a safe distance.

There is a saying in Judo, "to throw an opponent you must put yourself in a position to be thrown." It is the same with affairs of the heart. You can only be in a position to be loved if you are in a position to be hurt. 7s have trouble taking that gamble. This same thought process and fear of being taken advantage of can extend into any situation in which there are heavy demands or expectations. Fears can be reduced somewhat if the limits, rules, and expectations of a situation or relationship are laid out at the start.

To prevent a chain of perceived intrusions and betrayals from growing into fear or paranoia, the 7 views life as a string of snapshots. They are all related yet isolated. What happens tomorrow may not be what happened today under similar environments. This type of outlook where nothing is taken for granted lends itself to the skeptical posture of the 7. The 7 wants to know. They want to understand everything. They wish to be able to interpret everything. This is a way of defending themselves from their environment. Genius is to fuse knowledge, insight, and reality. Madness is when these oppose one another and a split occurs.

The 7 can go to either extreme. 7s can see patterns in things, and gain insight. They are able to relate things in one context to another context. Genius sees and recognizes patterns in things; madness imposes patterns on things, which leads to a distorted reality. In this they are like the 5. But unlike the 5 type, 7s may emphasize thinking over doing. Saying or doing reveals their position, and there may be a weakness there. It may be used against them. This is something that the 7 doesn't like to risk.

Many times this is because their words have been used against them by "trusted" friends or family. This balance has to be watched so that their mental world doesn't become all consuming. In the pursuit of pure ideas 7s do not want others to influence their thinking. (This seems to diminish their self-worth.) However, they tend not to totally trust their own ideas. If the 7 thinks that they are the only ones with the answers, they can drift into error by relying only on their unchecked ideas, and they can go further and further away from reality. They can project their anxieties and impulses onto their reality making them paranoid or off balance.

They are the Jungian introverted thinking types. This makes for too much subjectivity. The thoughts start with the subject and flow back to the subject. (This means that facts are collected in order to form a theory, and not for the facts themselves.) A better explanation is that the 7 is a subjective thinking type. 7s were ambivalent toward their parents, who may have nurtured them erratically.

They may have received conflicting signals in childhood such as parents who drank, partied, were in and out of church, or off and on as far as dependability. Even the stress of an unhappy family would lead to this feeling of ambivalence toward the parents and the world. The result is that the 7 lives in a constant state of alertness. They fear being controlled by others. They watch their environment and all in it in order to foresee trouble and protect themselves. Love/hate of parents and the world makes them detached; they retreat to their thoughts. There is a duality then between objective and subjective reality. This can lead to schizophrenia.

If the 7 is uptight they will have danger on their mind, but because they are looking for it they feel safer. 7s feel that if something can be seen (perceived), it can be understood, and mastered. They enjoy using knowledge. Ingenious, inventive, technical. Since there is always more to know, the 7 has trouble putting thoughts into action. They never feel comfortable with their level of knowledge since they realize that there is always more to know and learn. They fear the world yet are fascinated by it. The 7, like the 2, has a passive/aggressive streak. They will use silence and the withholding of their attention to control others. This is a good way of getting a point across and yet not disturbing their precious peace and quiet; they don't even have to display their suppressed emotions to do it. As a child they felt intruded upon. This could have been because they are very sensitive to noise and activity in their home, or because they could not get privacy because of a large, intrusive family, or small living space. They learned to "tune out" or hide out in order to find peace. The other family pattern is one in which there was abandonment so the child detached from his emotions and kept occupied mentally in his own world in order to survive. Their idea of controlling a situation is to stop reacting to it. Interaction drains them.

They take offense at having their time or energy put at others' disposal. 7s are often scholars of obscure fields. The expert in a field, having spent years compiling data, the 7s reclusive nature turns to feelings of isolation and loneliness if depression or enforced separation goes on too long. 7s have a feeling of superiority over those who like competition (as in sports), believing it to be a waste of time.

Since they are somewhat detached from their emotions, they need quiet time at the end of the day to sort out their feelings and wind down. They may calm down by thinking, reading, or working on projects. Since they are mind-centered, they connect with others through special interests or knowledge. They tend to interface with the world the same way. They are attracted to systems such as psychology, math, occult science, or natural science in order to explain and understand the world. At times they will realize how destructive this type of activity can be, especially to the insecure, but it is worth it to them to be able to secretly hurt someone without becoming actively emotionally involved. The superior function is intuitive, the inferior function is physical sensing.

Healthy 7s are visionaries, profound and comprehending thinkers. They love discovery. They are able to concentrate and become involved with a project. Innovative, genius, secure enough not to detach from their environment, and not cling to their own ideas. They have an open mind, with intuitive foresight. They are closer to being contemplative than thinkers. They can convey ideas and information in simple, clear form. Wise, knowledgeable, and dignified. They have a sense of the self and the universe in an inner-active role. Interest and research in philosophy, psychology, science, and mysticism. Able to observe, analyze, draw conclusions and applications. Specialized fields, scientific and research writings. Needs time to be alone and to sort out the acquired data and associated thoughts of the day.

The average 7 is intellectual, analytical, and specialized. Making a science of things, research, and scholarship. Can be detached. Enjoys speculating on ideas and theories. They tend to interpret everything around a pet theory which may lead to extremes. 7s can be eccentric. They can make a "science" out of everything. They may break things down to study so much that the big picture is lost. They are bookish. Intellect is their forte'. There may have been a lonely period in their childhood which urged them to turn more toward their mind. They tend to be high-strung. Their thoughts flow in a stream from one thing to another in a chain of seemingly (to the observer) unrelated thoughts. This takes their conversation over a scattered, branching, detailed path at times. Their thoughts may be hard to follow.

The unhealthy 7 can be reclusive and isolated from reality. Cynical, aggressive, and obsessed with strange ideas. Phobias, paranoia, schizophrenia, genius gone to insanity. Nothing is certain because every angle is examined, and all things are possible. They may think that one grand idea holds the key to all answers. Or they may reduce things to such a point the awe is gone and the truth is lost. They love to take ideas to the limits, sometimes for the shock value. They can become antagonistic with anyone who disagrees with them since this actually threatens their reality. If you look you will find fault. They are rejected because of their ideas and self-righteous attitudes, and so feel contempt for others. Ignorance, skepticism, fear, dishonesty, melancholia, pessimism, false pride, sarcasm, mental disorders, uncontrolled anger.

7s will act out by retreating into a shell. A nervous recluse that is hiding from the world. They escape into imaginations and fantasy worlds which have their foundations in the mind. Feelings of betrayal can drive them further in. A person that is hyper-sensitive to activity, noise, and environmental disorder produces a snappy, grumpy, silent hermit. The basis is the fear of not being able to take it all in and protect themselves from a hostile environment.

7s need to let go of isolating themselves, rejecting others, snobbishness, thinking that others cannot be depended on, cynicism, feeling powerless, violated, feeling taken advantage of, suspicion, aloofness, deviousness, and lying. The 7 must focus on their ability to find the truth, their fine mind, ability to reason, sense of class or elegance, ability to research, strategies, spiritual insights, feel for the metaphysical, science, medicine, math, the occult, and to teach others.

7s will work out by balancing physical and mental activity. Develop a sense of humor. Accept the fact that you can't know everything or see everything coming so you might as well relax and laugh at it.

Enneagram 6s:

Desires to be safe, protected, give and receive support, and guidance

Fears being abandoned by an authority figure, without backup or support, and not belonging to the larger group

Feels anxious and vulnerable

Skeptical about the intentions of others

Prefers stability and a tried-and-true way of doing things

They need a peaceful, safe, secure home

Worries often about possible negative events

They fear being unprepared for issues and problems

Will test people. They do not automatically trust people

They are, devoted, loyal, and faithful to those they deem worthy of their inner circle

Never makes hasty decisions

They are disciplined and organized

Don't want to be in charge but they do make great teammates

Usually more on the conservative side. They do not like taking risks

They are careful with financial decisions

Numerology 6

Type 6 respects loyalty. They will watch and test others and their attitudes before they will trust them. They have to watch their feelings of anxiety and insecurity. This is a type full of contradictions. They want trust but they test others first before trusting. They honor authority yet fear it. They do not like aggression yet are at times aggressive. They search for security yet feel insecure. They fear being rejected yet will reject others if they do not measure up to their moral and social value structure. Anxiety causes this vacillation. They feel more secure with "big brother" to watch out for them, be it the corporation, political party, or church. They need something to trust and believe in.

They want approval from others but resist being in positions of inferiority. They fluctuate from obedience to rebellion; likable to cranky and snappy. They are actually in conflict with both internal authority (superego) and outward authority. They tend to look outside of themselves for direction, yet don't like being in a subservient position. They can be openly hostile to an authority figure if the distrust or anger at the father has built up. They will appear rebellious and defiant at the authority figure as there is a transference of feelings acquired in childhood. We should again point out that there are two sides to the 6.

We see conformity and rebellion; honor and anger occurring in the same person. Sometimes they happen at the same time causing fear and loyalty, love and hate to come into a dynamic balance in the 6, and it is all based around the father image. Almost always the child tried to love the father even though he may have been demanding or unfair. This did not leave a way to deal sufficiently with the negative feelings. As the child tried harder to reach a level of approval in the parent's eyes, anger built because of the harsh, disciplinarian, or unapproachable posture that the father operated from. It may have been a morally high or correct issue, but the way it was enforced did not convey love. This sends a double message to the child.

First it says that it is very important to do the right and just thing, to be loyal and good. But secondly, it forms an image of fear and suspicion in regard to authority figures. This forms a push-pull relationship. This tension forms the basis of their anxiety. When it builds, they want the security they missed, but since they have come to trust in only themselves on the deeper level, they reject the authority on an inner level and either can become aggressive and belligerent or try to serve and placate to assure the authority's continued goodwill and protection.

6s are an introverted feeling type. They, like the 8 type, want to be the protector. 6s are more parental in this quest than the bossy 8. Also, like the 8, they are looking for someone to be their protector. The 6 is looking for a guardian or father image to trust and rely on. Isn't it fitting and reasonable that the things that we seek to be are the very things that we are looking for in others?

So many times we could learn from ourselves if we would recognize that the simply stated truth of a song holds the key, "and in the end, the love you take will be equal to the love you make." We should carry it further and say that what we need, are missing, and hope to find is what we try to become for ourselves, and for others. It is just another way of trying to fulfill our own needs. When all is said and done, that's all we can rely on anyway.

6s emotionally tend to swing and are hard to anticipate. They may like someone, then become concerned about being taken advantage of, and withdraw in suspicion. This brings in their anxiety and the need for reassurance, so back to the person they may go for assurance.

The 6 child identified positively with the father image. They gained identity and security by being approved by them. Anxiety arose if approval wasn't forthcoming. They learned that by following rules, and being responsible and obedient, they gained positive strokes from the father image, and this strengthened their feelings of worth and security. If they did not please this authority, 6s learned that retribution would come. This means that they have a very strong super-ego. In time this father image is transferred to other authorities such as law, business, government, and husband.

They fear being left, so they place great value on long-term relationships. Family is the symbol of the emotional stability and commitment that 6 stands for. If they veer into disobedience, they will worry about what others think. There is a fear that others will turn on them.

The superior function is emotional-feeling, and the inferior function is mental-thinking. There is a need to be the authority so that there is less authority over you, coupled with a need to serve and be protected by an authority image leads some 6s into being police officers, nurses, doctors, preachers, priests, or managers.

There are two distinct directions a 6 might choose based on which most affected them, the moral and loyalty issue, or harshness and authoritarianism. They can seek to serve and protect the moral standards, or they can rebel against authority and become lawless, or mafia types, serving another kind of group or family. It isn't surprising that 6s are likely to be involved in long-term relationships. Their loyalty and tenacity can allow them to survive a long time even in a dysfunctional relationship.

Healthy 6s are reliable, trustworthy, loyal, trusting, and independent yet cooperative. They take commitment seriously. They elicit strong emotional responses from others. They will fight for you as they would for themselves. Good natured, good sense of humor, friendly, a parent image (if they try to emulate their father image within). Capable of 50-50 relationships. They are good leaders since they know what others are looking for in authority. They can reassure others, and be emotionally open, loving, and caring.

6s lost faith in authority as children. Something in the parents' actions spawned fear and feelings of being powerless or overpowered. The parent may have had traits such as an explosive temper or trying to hide some secret that made the child feel that they were untrustworthy. This is carried over to adulthood in the form of hesitancy to act, and suspicion of authority. They tend to doubt their own ability. The anti-authoritarian stance forms a split path.

On one hand, it makes them gravitate to the underdog. They will go to extremes to beat the odds, from heroism or even martyrdom in the search to beat the system, pull together, and set things right that the authorities have screwed up. This is the rebellious stance. It is fueled by feelings of oppression and anger from past misuse by authorities. This can be summed up by a "you and me against the world" attitude.

The other path is one of being devoted to an authority figure or group, as long as the 6 feels that the group or authority is going in the correct direction. They become loyal servants, able to follow a chain of command well. They are dutiful public servants, parental types. This is a strange type of self-protection. They like serving, and therefore affecting others. This is because they think that if they are on your side, they won't be harmed. 6s are afraid of being ganged up on or harmed by an unexpected turn of others. So, they serve the more powerful group or person in exchange for their protection. This type of 6 tries to do what is right in society's eyes. 6s do not give in order to get something back. They give in order to feel safe. They fear betrayal.

This is also a person who fears intimacy. They can easily project their fears and suspicions onto their partner, accusing them of not wanting to be close, or that they are in doubt of their true feelings and intentions. 6s need to know that their partner has respect and faith in them. They need to know that their partner feels safe with them. This is because this is what the 6 is in need of, so they will try to project their needs onto the partner. They will bask in the reflection of the feelings of the partner spawned by the 6. These are feelings of "nesting" in a safe place. This is what the 6 wants to feel first-hand.

This should be a lesson to all of us that we all tend to live assuming that others feel, need, and want the same as we do. This narrow view can lead to misunderstandings and wasted time. We must all learn to see things from other points of view. Real communication is speaking to people on their own level and from their own point of view. 6s should be careful not to project these feelings on to others to make them see ulterior motives that are harmful to the 6. This even goes for their mates. Because of the background of the cause of this number, it is difficult for 6s to trust and be intimate without fear. Yet they need and want closeness and have the capacity to feel deeply.

Healthy 6s are devoted and protective without being meddlesome. They are interested in being patient and fair. Truth, justice, and the American way are the battle cry for the healthy 6. They are domestic, reliable, tenacious, and conservative. They are good listeners, and therefore good teachers, counselors, and ministers. Education is important to them.

Average 6s identify with authority figures and follow their lead. They are traditionalists, family, and company people. The 6 is dutiful and responsible. 6s on this level begin to show contradictions in personality. They are ambivalent and passive/aggressive. They want authority over them in order to feel more secure, yet they fight against authority and rebel at times. They may become defensive, authoritarian, partisan, and blame others if things go wrong. This is an overcompensation for their fear and insecurity. This fear may be seen in the 6 becoming dependent, even comfortable being ordered around. This vacillation between dependence and independent leadership urges makes them very unstable. When they make decisions, they are likely to look for precedents such as rules, regulations, and scriptures. This adds to their security.

Unhealthy 6s are insecure and dependent. Anxiety and feelings of inferiority are high. They are sadistic. They overreact due to insecurities. Archie Bunker types, fraught with prejudices, bigotry, and blustering. Trying to recreate the security that they had in the past themselves, to no avail. They overcompensate for their fear and insecurity by becoming tyrants. They deal harshly with the mistakes of others while letting themselves off the hook.

Everything becomes a crisis because of insecurity. Things are blown out of proportion. It ends in masochism in which the 6 seeks union with others in a twisted way by saying, "I've been bad, I didn't follow all of the rules, punish me so that you can love me again." If there isn't punishment, they will punish themselves in order to try and substitute their punishment for a punishment that they fear would be more severe from the authority. If this isn't enough they will provoke the authority by turning to sadism. Meddlesome, irresponsible, unyielding, self-righteous, a tyrant.

6s will act out through a rebellion and hardness that hides a fear of authority. They will have a quick, judgmental temper. A tyrant-like need to bully or control hides a fear of being abandoned, misused, or persecuted.

The 6 must let go of their fear of abandonment, feeling trapped by obligations, anxieties and worry about themselves and others, judging others, a tough facade to hide feelings, being negative about situations or people, the need to boss or mother others, and stubbornness. They need to focus on their abilities to guide and care about others, to serve the family or community, have true concern for others, a nurturing heart, and a parental sense of fairness.

The 6 will work out by realizing that no one can take control or exert authority over them - that is something that has to be given. They are safe to be their own authority. Be secure with yourself, and you will find security in others.

Enneagram 7s:

Desires freedom, happiness, spontaneity, to be carefree

Fears being tied down, restricted, trapped, limited in choices, or bored

They fear the pain that comes from simply living

They will avoid pain and responsibility when possible

Sevens dislike routines and ruts

Dislikes being limited; they will think outside the box and innovate

They are always looking for new experiences to feel excited about

Avoids environments that are hostile or given to conflicts or disagreements

They want to relax, party, meet, talk, and exchange ideas

May have several interests and hobbies to keep their minds occupied

They are curious, spontaneous and annoyingly child-like at times

They like to jest, tease, joke and laugh

They are all about exercising their free will

They are funny, fun loving, and the life of the party

As stated before, the types 5 and 7 are reversed between the systems of Enneagram and Numerology. To keep the data synchronized, the numerology types have been reversed for the ease of reading and understanding the parallels between the systems.

Numerology 5

Type 5 wants to be happy and to escape anxiety. They will do this by experiencing and getting "acquainted" with as many things as possible. Because of this they are considered the "generalist." They have a wide range of knowledge and experience.

5s tend to act in the immediate. This usually leads to more doing since one action or search will lead to another. This type does not think about conscience very much. In extreme cases, they could be somewhat sociopathic since they are involved with immediate gratification. Being the extroverted sensation type, their frame of reference is the "real" world of sensory data. Input is direct from the environment to the person, more so than other types. This sets them up for becoming an addictive personality. They will consume more than they need and need more than they can possibly appreciate, feeling that the world exists to fulfill their appetites.

If they are balanced, they will get great joy out of life and its experiences. Their thrust is toward productivity; however, if their focus shifts it will go from producing to possessing. This is where experience becomes consumption. They will then stay busy trying to keep their sensations high. But this creates a type of narcotic effect which demands more, better, faster, and longer stimulation. This will bring the 5 to overextend himself. Not finding happiness through these experiences, they become insecure, unhappy, and anxious. At this point they will become enraged and desperate, claiming that they have been in some way deprived of happiness, unfairly so. They will lash out at those who deny them. In public 5s tend to be charming, and disarming.

As children, they escaped into a world of imagination. 5s don't broadcast anxiety, they look happy and lighthearted. They love playing and planning. 5s are likely not to worry much. They are a perpetual Peter Pan. This gives way to a type of narcissism. They love new adventures. They view the world with infinite possibilities and become nervous at the idea of losing an option or narrowing their possibilities. This is why they tend to make commitments with "back doors." They always want an alternate plan. They are masters at going with the flow, as long as the flow doesn't limit their personal freedom. This, to a 5, is the greatest sin.

5s have the ability to see connections between seemingly unrelated ideas, methods, and disciplines. They have unique abilities of problem solving. Inventive and imaginative, they possess the ability to synthesize unusual veins of knowledge. They must refrain from rationalizing escapism and boredom. Some 5s like escapism and having fun so much that instead of acquiring things they will use their money to get away, or just have fun. They approach relationships by sharing life experiences, especially the good ones.

This seems to confirm their own experiences, memories, and feelings, and in some way validate them just that much more. The 5 seems to feed off the experience, and the other person's reaction simply expands the feast. It also reflects back to the 5 the way that they already feel. Here is a problem, however. With all of this living behind them, they are likely to become jaded and unflappable. At this point, the

5 can get in trouble. They are apt to become apathetic or depressed, or, in seeking a better high, they can turn to drugs, drink, sex, or any high to break the monotony of the same old excitement.

If a 5 is in a restrictive situation, for instance a bad marriage, they will become moody, cranky, angry, and even suicidal, as they blame others for holding back their freedom. If you can hold a 5 by keeping their interest, marriage to a 5 can be interesting. It should consist of a lot of activity, food, fun, travel, and sex.

They seem to be given to situational ethics as they go through life seeking what feels good. This is doubly true when it comes to love, which they can easily confuse with sex. They will rationalize their actions by saying, "But I love her, so what else counts?" It is difficult for 5s to be tied to needy or emotionally dependent people unless they are along for the ride and don't tie the 5 down. The 5, like the 1, finds it hard to take blame. Confrontation and accusations bring a loud inner voice of failure. Since they use others' opinions or desires of them as a meter of their self-worth, this affects the basis of their worth in their own eyes. It is good they can divert their attention easily so that something bad can be covered up by something good fairly quickly so that the pain doesn't last long.

5s have good memories of childhood, but this may be because they tend to focus on the happy side of things. They don't usually cleave to hate or resentment very long. There is a slight tendency to be closer to the mother in childhood. There is also a rebellion against authority that would tie them down to work, or commitment. 5s hate boredom. They usually have several projects going on at the same time. They will go from one to the other seeing parallels and similarities between all of them. Casual commitments are made easily, but permanent commitments are hard. (They scare them a great deal.)

5s want a little taste of everything that is best. They are gluttons for experience. They tend to think of more than one thing at a time. They do this by putting an unsolved problem on the back burner while working out a second problem. At some time, the foreground problem will, in some way, spark a connection with the background issue, and the answer will bubble up to the conscious mind. This is just one way that one thing is in some way bound up or connected to another. They love talking, intellectualizing, and brainstorming. If given a new fact, 5s will try to fit it into many different scenarios. This leads to a viewpoint that sees the interdependence and interrelationships of things.

They are editors, writers, communicators, linguists, philosophers, and idea people. Eternally young (and sometimes immature), they love doing and experiencing but fear having their projects judged. Because of their charm and ability to communicate, they can lead others to believe that their knowledge has more depth than it truly has. In fact, they have a wide base of knowledge, but usually not a lot of depth.

At their worst they can be charlatans. They are afraid of being revealed as less than what they appear to be. They are happy with situations in which no one is above or below them, and all are on the same level. They are good at promoting ideas, and networking with others.

5s were formed in part by a negative orientation to the mother image. Due to any of a number of reasons from poverty, war, illness, divorce, or simply her own nature such as neglect, smothering, or passive/aggressive control, she frustrated the child. The child found himself not being nurtured and secure. The child then tries to get his needs met and nurture himself. He did this from the world and its experiences. This substitutes for a mother's love. The id is stuck in instant gratification, and they place no restraints on themselves, denying themselves nothing. The superior function is physical or sensing, the inferior function is intuitive.

Healthy 5s concern themselves with satisfying their true needs. They add to the world, not consume it. They are productive, have great memories and minds, as well as large areas of knowledge. Healthy 5s assimilate reality and experiences into themselves. They affirm life and are joyous, full of wonder and reverence. The spiritual life becomes a reality to them. They acquire faith and look for the good in things and people. They will be swept into an awareness of the metaphysical. The inner world of the 5 is made up of impressions. It is a catalogue of experiences. They are multifaceted. They usually have refined tastes and a sophisticated air to them. Language and writing skills aren't uncommon. They are very observant and have quick, dry senses of humor. Adaptable, active, resourceful, versatile, curious, investigative, sensual, sexual, and able to take a chance.

Average 5s have a vibrant love of life. They want to try it all. To perceive it is to know and enjoy it. They pay attention to the finer things of life, such as food, clothes, music, and sex. They can be elegant people. They are "oral" people. Most of their activities deal with appetites and mouth. There is something of the comedian or performer in the five, usually driven by insecurity. They are sassy and irreverent. Their brashness may offend some, but others find it refreshing and humorous. They are not subtle people and can be tactless, simply speaking their minds. They tend to push activities and experiences past the bounds of good taste. They may be manic, high on their illusion of life as if on speed, full of grandiose plans, none of which are carried out.

Unhealthy 5s are jealous of what others have. They are wasteful. Excess rings in their lives. (You can never be too rich or too thin.) They started out getting high on life, but now life can't offer enough, not even in excess, so they turn to alcohol, drugs, and debauchery. Not even T.V. or food is safe from this. They become jaded and insatiable. Unhealthy 5s stay in motion. Since all of their "reason" is turned extroverted, they can't figure out why they are unhappy. They become indiscriminate in their desires and consumptions; depravity is the order. They are unhappy and this feeling is directed toward the mother image who did not nurture them, so they act like spoiled children, since the id is frozen in that time.

They act out, doing and saying things to hurt others without concern or restraint. Having wasted their energy, they slow down and become very depressed, even suicidal. Given to excesses, over-indulgence, addictions, impulsiveness, and restlessness. Fickle, critical, discontent, noncommittal.

The 5 will act out by impulsive, consumptive behavior. They will accuse, blame, and strike out at others to hide their own frustrations. The frustration and unhappiness of not being satisfied by anything for very long time drives them toward more and more until they are stopped by addictions, compulsions, or exhaustion. Fear of losing their personal freedom can lead to lying, adultery, and lack of commitment.

The 5 needs to let go of recklessness, impulsiveness, addictions, not taking responsibility, venting frustration on others, burnout, need for instant gratification, impatience, escapism, lack of self-discipline or restraint, and overextending self. They need to focus on their quick mind, ability to communicate ideas, charisma, spontaneity that energizes others; plus, their ability to motivate and investigate, their curiosity, sense of humor, and resilience.

5s will work out by realizing once and for all that any happiness that comes through the senses is transitory at best. All ups will have an equal down, so it is best to seek the center path. Commitment to someone you love will keep you from losing them and having to look for a "second best" for the rest of your life. To be willingly committed is not to be bound, it is only to love. You don't need a back door if you really mean the commitment.

Enneagram 8s:

Desires to govern themselves, to be independent and free of higher authorities, not reliant

Fears being weak, powerless, without authority of their own, and put in a vulnerable situation

Aggressive, domineering, and strong personalities

They are motivated by wealth and position

Self-reliant

They prefer to be in control, the boss, owner, or director

They do things on their own

Serious, stubborn, and confident

They are powerful and willful personalities

Has stamina and mental strength

They thrive in challenges and adversities

Decisive, they do not like to be questioned

Even though they see vulnerability as weakness, they will protect the weak and submissive

They want efficiency and will modify or create a system in order to get it

Can appear angry or arrogant because they are so intense

Numerology 8

8 types want to be self-reliant, to act in their own self-interest, and to make an impact on people and their environment. Love of power is the love of self. They attempt to conform the environment, and those in it, to their aims. They relate to the environment in order to prevail over it. They take charge, imposing their will. Getting their way is very important to them. The 8's sense of self is stronger than their sense of others. They are steely and single minded. They are the extroverted intuitive type.

They have a keen sense of things in the making. They are always seeking new possibilities. Stable conditions suffocate them. They cannot be frightened away from a new possibility, even if it goes against previous convictions. They are the champion of the underdog. They are confident that by their will they can reach their goals. Although this presentation may sound harsh, if motivated correctly it will yield experts, athletes, and gold-medal contenders. However, if they go astray, they usually get caught up in their own egotism. They can't see or believe that there is anything wrong with them, even though they may not take the needs or wants of others into consideration.

One possibility of the formation of the 8 type is as follows: the 8 may have learned that one parent in their life did not respond to them unless they asserted themselves. This assertiveness may have had to increase to aggression from time to time until the child got his attention and his way. They learned that a strong-willed child could dominate even an adult.

Soon this same process was used in other areas of their life in ways of being aggressive and strong even if they were wrong in order not to face the fact, or punishment for doing wrong. They then began to walk on others' feelings. If the ego is unchecked, they will view life only as power and its use, so they will take advantage of any weakness they see.

The preferred position is to charge in, take control, and maintain it. 8s believe that the truth comes out in a fight. A clean fight is exhilarating to them. They feel that anger, fighting, intimacy, and truth are all related.

The 8s tough exterior covers a heart of a child that had to fight for his space. They would like to stop fighting, but they don't trust others to take control and be just. Blaming and punishing the wrong-doers is a preoccupation with 8s. They have an all-or-nothing way of approaching things. Security to an 8 means knowing all of a situation and having power over things. The 8 may say that if they know all of the facts, they can have the proper response and emotional posture for it. The 8 is intent on power or control. Power can be in the form of money, possessions, people or simply control.

Another possibility of the formation of an 8 is one of hard knocks and simple survival. Because of a parent who was a disciplinarian, harsh, or emotionally distant the 8 may have difficulty in expressing the vulnerable side of themselves. This is a childhood scenario of being pushed around, treated unjustly, and ignored by a parent, sibling, or friends.

A bad school, a tough part of town, or a poor childhood could exacerbate a survival instinct. The feeling was that the person in control did not act with the child's best interests in mind. There could have been a divorce or other situation involving a parent's harshness or anger that the child took personally. It damaged the child's faith in their authority and security figures. They learned that the world was not safe. The 8 child had to be old enough to stand on his own or think for himself in order to become self-reliant. This means that at least part of the mistreatment should have occurred between the ages of 6 and 16. There could have been a simple but definite disagreement and an emotional parting of ways.

Another possibility of the formation of the 8 type which can, at times, exist side by side with the other patterns is as follows. This type can be caused by one parent turning the child against the other parent by having no faith or anything good to say about them. This suspiciousness can also be caused by a parent or adult abusing, neglecting, or molesting the child. This disregard for the child's welfare makes the child suspicious of them. So now the 8 feels that he should be in control because he has been taught not to trust the authority figure. They think that they can do it better than others, and they will protect not exploit others. Yet, due to their strong personality and will, at times they can do just that by running rough shod over those of less strength.

No matter how the 8 was formed they can become so focused on a goal that they can deny pain, fatigue, opposition, and even the odds that are against them. It does not let them see what is enough, or even their own limits. At times it can go so far as to create a type of tunnel vision. The 8 will not see the full picture. They can repress feelings and even incoming data until the truth overtakes them. When they are knocked down by it, they realize that the signs were there all of the time. They may even find that others' ideas, opinions, or views simply annoy them.

The 8 is the type of the judge since they demand justice. They always want the wrong doers to be punished and vengeance to be done. It is always their justice that they try to impose on others so they appear to be judgmental. They can be irritable and dogmatic. If the 8 is not balanced, the right and wrong of a situation will get totally lost in the goal to win the argument. 8s are very competitive, even in discussions. It is difficult for them to restrain their expression, whether it be anger, sex, or competitiveness. They are a consumptive type. They can be classified as loners. Although it might not be their preference, it is what is easiest for them. They become attached in slow painful steps; steps of testing and trials for the mate.

They value open honest arguments. If you can't take anger expressed in your face, don't pick an 8. They will test the mate to see if they can dominate them. If they can, they won't respect them as much. (This is much like the 1) Once trust is established, there is a bonding that is very deep. We can see why 8s would not be so good at diplomacy or "sweet-talk." They aren't emotionally attuned, and if they think that you aren't being up front about everything, they will attack. The attack comes from an insecurity that they are being blind-sided or manipulated, and a feeling of frustration of having to waste energy on things as frivolous as emotions. Especially when it can all be avoided if all of the cards were really put on the table.

The 8, like the 1, hates being wrong. One of the favorite tricks of the 8 who has been caught in a situation where they are wrong or have made bad choices is to attack first. Accusations will be directed to the innocent party. They will often pick an area of the other party's behavior that can be brought into question so that the discussion will be re-directed away from their weakness. The sad thing is that the 8s pride may be such that they refuse to inspect their own behavior. 8s will let you know exactly where you stand, and they expect the same. They are possession, power, and territory-driven, and that goes for work as well as romance.

The mature 8 will have learned to give a little and meet in the middle. They have an overriding fear of having to submit and depend on others, probably because they did not think that they could depend on one of the parents without a fight of will or being taken advantage of. 8s grew up in a situation of having to fight for their rights. It could have been a physical fight such as with siblings or other kids. Or it could have been a fight of wills. The child may have had to simply set his mind that the situation would not break his spirit.

8s don't like compromise. They tend to view things as black and white. The middle ground leaves them feeling vulnerable. The superior function is mental-thinking, the inferior function is emotional-feeling.

Healthy 8s are magnanimous, self-restrained, courageous, self-assertive, confident, and inspiring. A leader and authoritarian. Self-restraint means not kicking people when they are down; knowing what and when things are appropriate and restraining self until then. They can better the lives of others. Benefactor, visionary. They can thrive on and learn from adversity and turning setbacks into opportunities. They can create and maintain social order, material success and personal achievements. They are fair, ethical, and responsible for their actions, especially as others are concerned.

Average 8s are enterprising, rugged, forceful, aggressive, dominating, willful, intimidating, combative, and belligerent. The builder or the power broker. They think that there can only be one person on top, and they are it. They are not team players. They are the entrepreneurs, businessmen (or women), and political movers and shakers. They are the self-made man. Money is the means to the end of being self-sufficient so as to not depend on others. They are negotiators (buy, sell, trade, make a buck).

They love risk, danger, and excitement especially in the financial world. To make money is to make more of themselves. Female 8s tend to dominate their mates since they have the same ego structure as the male 8. Cultural restraints stand in their way however. 8 men are ambivalent toward women, seeing them as they had their mothers. They tend to dominate them, even becoming aggressive. They can easily become womanizers. 8s describe a combative childhood, a situation where the strong survived. They learned to protect themselves by becoming sensitive to the intentions of others. They grow to ignore the odds, and even become blind to the issues at times, as they pursue a goal single mindedly. They come to think of themselves as the righter of wrongs, the enforcer of justice. Fairness, justice, and control are the central issues.

Unhealthy 8s are relentless, ruthless, vengeful, violent, megalomaniacs, and intimidating. Only money seems to be reliable to them; even the love of friends and family is secondary to power, control, or money. Their view is so narrow that they are blind to what they and their demands inflict on others. Their pride will not allow them to examine the possibility of being wrong, much less admit it. This same pride and need to be in control makes them refuse to ask for help from anyone. They have very poor judgment when it comes to others and their emotional needs. They use and hurt people and are blind to everything other than seeing the thing they wanted done was done in their way.

Unhealthy 8s are viewed as unstable. They begin to believe their own bloated image of themselves. They swagger and bluster and are self-important. They hate softness (weakness) in themselves and even more so in others. It is viewed as weakness. From their perspective, might makes right. Treacherous and immoral, they will do whatever they have to do to reach their goal, including violence. The more power a person has the less need a person has to justify themselves; therefore, the acquisition of power is a means of combating guilt. The more the 8 sinks into megalomania the more they are likely to think that they are above the law, and even the instrument of God, or God himself.

8s will act out through aggression and a bid to control the environment and all that are in it. They will be bossy to the point of rage and physically compel others to obey if necessary. If a person resists, they will escalate their effort until someone gets hurt, all in the name of control. 8s need to let go of abusiveness and anger toward others, trying to control or bully others. They need to stop the bossiness and thinking that theirs is the only way.

They obsess about perfection in performance to the point of becoming angry if someone falls short. They are hard hearted, thinking that everyone is incompetent. They fear being controlled by others, letting pride, ego, or coldness come between them and the ones that they really care for. They force their way on others by greed and intimidation. The 8s need to focus on their ability to know the potential of people and help them achieve it. They have the ability to organize to make people's lives easier. They know how to make and manage money in order to give and share. 8s can be very philanthropic. They have the ability to inspire confidence and leadership. They have the ability to manage and direct.

8s will work it out by allowing themselves to feel, and put themselves in the shoes of others. They should ask themselves if they would like to be hurt, yelled at, hit, demoralized, or abused? Then why do it to others? They don't have to be correct and in control all of the time. Do unto others as you would have them do unto you! Remember?

Enneagram 9s:

Desires peace, harmony, status quo, untroubled by strife

Fears conflict, emotional tension, being rejected or disowned, loss of peace, breaking the status quo, and dealing with the emotionally unknown or combative situation.

Wants to avoid conflict at the cost of their own feelings

Likely to procrastinate

They crave a peaceful environment and emotional comfort

They avoid doing things that cause turmoil

They often ignore things that they do not like, even though they may have to live with them on a daily basis

A gentle soul, they love listening to and helping others

Forgiving

Long suffering

They may feel emotionally overwhelmed in times of stress, that can cause them to shut down, stop, and procrastinate

Easy going, but they hate being controlled and will rebel. That is the line of their temper

Spiritual, connecting with nature and seeing the connection with all things

Numerology 9

9 wants union, harmony, and peace. They want to preserve the status quo. Tension and conflict are to be avoided. They tend to ignore things that upset them. Their sense of self comes from being in union with others. Their view of life is open and optimistic. This causes an easy-going attitude that doesn't see the need to change things. They may even ignore the wrong that is staring them in the face. They are a relating type but they have a hard time relating to reality. 9s tend to blur their own identity because they want

union with another. They may not reach their full potential because of this.

To better conform to others, the 9 represses part of self. They equate self-assertiveness with aggression, so they have difficulty expressing themselves as they should. They are the introverted sensation type. They are conspicuously calm and passive. This is because there is a kind of detachment from reality.

The formation of the 9 type seems to have two patterns that run sequentially. The identification with the parent image was comfortable for them. Early childhood was a comparatively idyllic time that the person would like to recapture. In the second part of the sequence or the second scenario, the later period of childhood could have been shattered by illness, death, or divorce of a parent. This propels the id to try to hold on to its better days where union and reliance on another met all of their needs.

Many 9s may have been close to their grandparents and felt a parental bond with them, especially in their early childhood. This love could have filled the void of a missing parent and provided for the emotional needs of the child. (I have noticed a very high percentage of 9 Souls come from broken homes.) In many of these instances the grandfather took the place of the father. If there was not a divorce there may have been abuse (either emotional or physical). This to the child, is tantamount to an emotional divorce. (Normally these emotional changes would have occurred between ages 4 and 9.)

In another scenario the 9 child was overlooked. Their needs, opinions, and point of view were not taken into account. At times, when they expressed a view they were told to shut up, or that their opinion was stupid. Their ideas were ignored. After too much of this, the 9s began to repress their feelings, preferences, and feelings.

They let others make the choices for them. They develop a keen sense of what others want. A type of emotional diplomacy keeps them from going against the flow and being reminded that their opinion doesn't count. That is always very hurtful. They take comfort in small physical comforts. They began to emotionally withdraw as they learned that nothing helped their cause, not even anger. They try to set up ways of not having to choose by setting up routines and operating on a kind of ritual.

9s try to operate through this numbness to the effect that they have trouble keeping their minds on things or sticking to things. 9s "feel" their memories, they are so strong. Therefore, they are not likely to fade, and neither are any grudges they may have. They are not fully in touch with any feelings they have. It is almost as if a partial filter is set up. Anger is one way that the wants and wishes become revealed. They may say, "I didn't realize that I felt so strongly about that." Without this direction it leads to scattered energy, teetering, and not being able to direct and motivate themselves over a long period.

9s are very susceptible to inertia. They have trouble with commitment and follow-through. They feel a need to keep the status quo. They will go to extremes so as not to act or change things. This goes for relationships, situations, and even things about themselves. This can cause serious problems in relationships as the 9 "flakes out."

They can't come to a firm decision because they were emotionally punished for it as a child. In one scenario of a 9s childhood, the parent viewed the child's wants as an intrusion or an interference with their desires. The parent then ignored or chastised the child for having desires that might conflict with the parent's wishes. The parent could have been selfish, or given to "martyrdom." Yet, on the positive side, this has forced them to develop the ability to see all sides of a situation. We must realize that repressed feelings and preferences are like water – they will always seek a way out. This lends itself to a number of passive-aggressive strategies. One is to take control by being late. This puts others on your time schedule. Another is to refuse to make up your mind or make a commitment. This puts others temporarily under your control since they are waiting on you to decide. (That is, until they get mad and give up in anger.) 9s can use their diplomatic sense (which allows them to know what others expect) against you, by simply not performing.

Healthy 9s are self-possessed and fulfilled. They are content, optimistic, emotionally stable, supportive, good natured, and unpretentious, having overcome their fears of becoming an independent person, at one with themselves, even their aggressions. Able to bring more of themselves to others. They do not idolize others but are able to love realistically. Love of self and others can bring a mystical overtone. They have no guile and do not understand lying or cheating in others. They are positive and generous. They actively play a part in the cycle of life, growth, and death. It is embraced, and they age with dignity. They are idealistic, tolerant, giving, forgiving, compassionate, generous, and universal in their frame of thought. They are artists, thinkers, romantics, and universalists.

Average 9s are self-effacing, accommodating, passive, and minimize problems to appease others. Fatalistic, resigned to the fact that nothing can be done. They love to commune with others and nature. They love the outdoors: hiking, sailing, and camping. They have a mystical side, a magical, mythical sense of the world. Elves, fairies, and such are shown to others through them. The average 9 sees themselves through the eyes of others. This may cause them to subordinate themselves. They fear asserting themselves so they don't disrupt the perceived communion. They can begin to live for the other person.

They take the middle-of-the-road stance, morally and socially in order to be accepted. Respectability is very important to them because of this. They love the past and the old fashioned ways. They are nostalgic, sentimental, and take things at face value. They never want to upset the status quo. This is taken to such a degree that they tend to ignore negative things and say "Oh, we don't have to worry about that." They develop a happy-go-lucky outlook.

The next step is to detach themselves from reality and form a take it or leave it attitude. It is an easygoing style gone one step too far. They diminish their feelings and keep things on an even keel. Things don't sink in. This makes them part of the problem and not the solution. In relationships they idolize the other, then begin to substitute the idolized person for the real person. This makes them put less and less energy into the real relationship. They will do or promise whatever it takes to resolve a problem with others to appease them, but since they really do not want to deal with the problem, it isn't resolved and will show back up. The discussion has simply bounced off their heads. They have sacrificed their loved ones and friends to the need for peace, the status quo, and not dealing with reality. The superior function is intuitive, the inferior function is physical-sensing.

Unhealthy 9s are repressed, neglectful, obstinate, disassociated from reality, and possibly catatonic. Multiple personalities. There can exhibit a strange type of obstinate passivism in that they go too far to avoid conflict. They repress their aggression and become adamant about not facing problems. They flake out and sacrifice relationships, making others angry when they try to force the 9 to do anything about fixing a problem. They may strike out at the person, but more than likely, since they wish to maintain the status quo, they will be passive/aggressive. They will accuse the other person of causing trouble and making waves. They will use lines such as, "Everything will work out", "We've made it fine up to now", "You're making too much out of it", and "You're causing trouble and putting too much pressure on me." For people who do so little, 9s have less energy, probably because it is spent internally walling off reality. When reality does show its head because of their neglect, or having hurt someone through it, they will be plunged into despair, denial, and even suicide. They can become bitter, fickle, selfish, irresponsible, and given to emotional extremes.

9s will work it out by realizing their passive/aggressive behavior. Like the 2, you must dig to find your real motives. They will have a fiery temper if they are not in touch with their feelings. They need to see themselves as the peacemaker and altruist so badly that they will deny anger or its results. They will control by passive means, even to the extent that they will get satisfaction in seeing someone struggle. While they could help, they will stand by and do nothing. 9s carry grudges. Being flaky and forgetful when they don't want to face reality, even if it causes others to carry more than their share of the load.

The 9 should let go of believing that bad situations will just go away, ignoring unpleasant situations, being afraid of changing things, being emotionally detached, denying their own aggression and temper, not being in active control of their life, dependency, getting lost in doing the same routines and habits (this prolongs and promotes the numbness of life), living vicariously or pouring themselves into others in order not to face themselves or a situation, and having too many irons in the fire so that they don't have time to focus on themselves or problems.

The 9 should focus on their talent to give, altruism, intuition, far- reaching views, humanitarianism, art, acting, passion, ability to get in touch with feelings and truly live life, psychic ability, emotional content, the heart's light. 9s will work it out by getting a grip on how they really feel, and not playing silly games with others. Fight cleanly. Take an interest in the reality of things. Approach the world head on. Be dependable and straightforward when dealing with others. Above all, don't scatter your energy. Pick one thing and do it, then go to the next item.

Tips to Becoming a Better You

Checklist by the Numbers

This section is dedicated to listing the normal characteristics of each enneagram type and addressing common pitfalls of each type. Use this section as a quick reference for characteristics attached to each type.

Enneagram 1s:

High standard for their work and performance

Imposing standards on others

Serious and straightforward

Rude and unyielding

Principled and lives with strong moral values

Judgmental and critical

Rigid, stubborn, and resistant to change

Trailblazer, teacher, guide, inventor

Focused and attentive

Obsessive about the project at hand

Follows rules and regulations

Uses internal standards which are unexplained and unknown by others

Fears being imperfect

Judges others for being imperfect

Represses anger and frustrations

Vents anger by talking over people, arguing them down, and being overly critical

Tips for ones:

- Set practical, attainable goals and standards for yourself and those around you. Write these expectations down in clear, concise wording so that those around you can understand what you want and need.

- Practice mindfulness and meditation. Ones are highly driven but may come off as rude and single minded, especially when working in teams. Take time to put yourself in the shoes of others and understand how your actions and words impact those around you. You run the risk of demotivating the people around you when your language is overly critical. Be mindful. You will catch more flies with honey than vinegar.

- Express concerns soon after they enter your mind. Do not let negative emotions build up. Have open discussions about problems when they arise.

- Explore other people's opinions and points of view. Stay flexible in handling differences and remember not everything is objective. Keep in mind that there is always room for improvement. Your ways may work well, but you will improve much more quickly if you take time to explore what others have to say.

Enneagram 2s:

Helpful and inviting

Can be too trusting

Meaningful relations and connections are their first choice

They are selfless, devoted friends

They can be taken advantage of

Twos are great partners in life and business

They can impose themselves into situations to help, even when not wanted or invited

Can commit more than what is needed

They are generous, empathetic, and compassionate, sometimes to the point of losing themselves in others

Find joy in connecting with family and friends

Tips for Twos

- Take time to understand your own needs. Set clear boundaries with others around these needs. You will be able to help more people if you keep yourself healthy

- Learn to be comfortable accepting help from others. You can't pour from an empty cup. Remember, most people like helping other people. It makes them feel good about themselves. Accepting help when you need it will help you connect with your helper and give you more free time to connect with others around you.

- Take time away from others. Remember everyone needs their own space, some more than others. Use the time to analyze the thoughts and feelings of others without attaching them to your worth. Your usefulness does not equate to your worth.

Enneagram 3s:

Will strive for success

They will avoid being thought of as ordinary

Their motivation is high

They need the admiration of others to feel affirmed and worthy

Because they are the actor, their inner world does not match their outside face or actions

They can deceive themselves in their roles and lose themselves

They are always cognizant of how people view them

They are socially conscious about their presentation

Because they are driven to succeed, leadership comes naturally

Success is paramount because it reflects on their image

Can present a refined, graceful style, expensive tastes, cars, clothes, and food

They have high expectations of themselves and their place in society

Tips for Threes

- Be authentic. Do not let your natural need to stand out overtake your true personality. Take time to be yourself. Remember love attained through a cultivated image is not lasting.

- Take time to relax. You are more than your accomplishments. It is important to step back and enjoy life for what it is.

- Take time to build a network of people you can rely on. There is no such thing as a self-made man (or woman). Remember your accomplishments do not mean less if others help you get there and you accomplish so much more with a strong team than by yourself.

Enneagram 4s:

Feels they are different from others

They are introspective as they seek ways to emote and express

They are moody and can be unreliable when it comes to ordinary life

Their emotions and moods guide them so they may change perspectives often

Seek out those they believe understand them and they hate being lonely

Searches for a meaningful life and the meaning within life.

They seek respect and social recognition for their depth of feelings and expression

They are often disappointed when they discover that life does not care if they are special

In their dramatic life they attempt to find their real or ideal 'self', but they can lose themselves along the way

Feel that being melancholic and sad is part of the journey they are on

Tips for Fours

- Practice thinking objectively. Fours may spend too much time dwelling on feelings and emotions. It is critical to practice analytical thinking to keep in touch with the world around them.

- Stay present. Be careful not to spend too much time daydreaming about the future and appreciate the time you have now.

- Stay disciplined. This goes with daydreaming. Be mindful to produce results and work towards your goals, and do not romanticize the future too much.

Enneagram 5s:

Deep thinkers

Quiet, shy, introverted

Lost in thoughts

Absent-minded

Lacks focus in daily life due to inner distractions

Aloof, walled off emotionally

Can be highly knowledgeable in certain areas

Think many times before speaking

Does not work well in large groups and prefers to work alone

Mostly introverts

They hate small talk

They examine everything, and that includes long held ideas and beliefs

They do not care to maintain a status quo if it does not make sense or lacks proof

Tips for Fives

- Take time to invest in others. Fives may have a hard time nourishing their relationships, especially in stressful times. Make sure to avoid isolation and keep yourself out there.

- Get in touch with your emotions. Fives need to be careful not to over rationalize their emotions. When the question is "how do you feel?", overly analytical thinking can muddy the waters and deter you from pursuing what you want.

- Be present. Fives may live in their head too often, disconnecting them from the world around them. Work on turning your analytical brain off and being present with the ones around you.
-

Enneagram 6s:

Feels anxious and vulnerable

Skeptical about the intentions of others

Prefers stability and a tried and true way of doing things

They need a peaceful, safe, secure home

Worries often about possible negative events

They fear being unprepared for issues and problems

Will test people. They do not automatically trust people

They are devoted, loyal, and faithful to those they deem worthy of their inner circle

Never makes hasty decisions

They are disciplined and organized

Don't want to be in charge but they do make great teammates

Usually more on the conservative side. They do not like taking risks

They are careful with financial decisions

Tips for Sixes

- Trust others. Sixes are natural skeptics. They often have trouble trusting the people around them, even long-time partners. Sixes need to be mindful to avoid the urge to test those close to them.

- Stay positive. A Six's anxiety about the future may cause them to become compulsively negative. It is important for their relationships and their mental health that they stay mindful to look on the bright side of things.

- Stay mindful to manage emotions. Sixes often dwell on negative emotions. Their skeptical outlook and anxiety concerning the future can lead to depression and feelings of hopelessness. Sixes must be cautious not to feed into anxiety and depression

Enneagram 7s:

Fear being tied down, restricted, or bored

They fear the pain that comes from simply living

They will avoid pain and responsibility when possible

Sevens dislike routines and ruts

Dislikes being limited; they will think outside the box and innovate

They are always looking for new experiences to feel excited about

Avoids environments that are hostile or given to conflicts or disagreements

They want to relax, party, meet, talk, and exchange ideas

May have several interests and hobbies to keep their minds occupied

They are curious, spontaneous and annoyingly child-like at times

They like to jest, tease, joke and laugh

They are all about exercising their free will

They are funny, fun loving, and the life of the party

Tips for Sevens

- Think before you act. Sevens tend to make impulsive decisions. It is important for them to practice slowing down and weighing the consequences, especially when they are excited about the subject.

- Be patient and put off instant gratification. This is just another pitfall of impulsive decision making. Sevens need to be mindful to prepare for the future while they enjoy the present, remembering that quality often takes time

- Take time to listen to others. Sevens need for freedom can make them hyper independent and, as a result, less than accepting of others' opinions. They should be mindful to listen to the opinions of those around them and not misconstrue them as ploys against their independence.

Enneagram 8s:

Aggressive, domineering, and strong personalities

They are motivated by wealth and position

Self-reliant

They prefer to be in control, the boss, owner, or director

They do things on their own

Serious, stubborn, and confident

They are powerful and willful personalities

Has stamina and mental strength

They thrive in challenges and adversities

Decisive, they do not like to be questioned

Even though they see vulnerability as weakness, they will protect the weak and submissive

They want efficiency and will modify or create a system in order to get it

Can appear angry or arrogant because they are so intense

Tips for Eights

- Learn to give up control. Eights naturally crave control over situations. It is important they practice taking a back seat when the situation calls for it. One person is never the strongest in all areas. Keep in mind the best leaders delegate to the best people for the job. Learn to support those around you instead of attempting to control them.

- Explain your opinions and ask for forgiveness. Eights do not like to be questioned or challenged, often causing them to become overly assertive or aggressive. It is imperative for eights to practice resolving conflicts in a calm, non-aggressive, manner and to admit when they may have been wrong.

- Stay calm. Eights naturally respond to conflict and problems with anger. This can be unhealthy for them and demotivating for the people around them. They must be mindful to manage their anger and intensity.

Enneagram 9s:

Wants to avoid conflict at the cost of their own feelings

Likely to procrastinate

They crave a peaceful environment and emotional comfort

They avoid doing things that cause turmoil

They often ignore things that they do not like, even though they may have to live with them on a daily basis

A gentle soul, they love listening to and helping others

Forgiving

Long suffering

They may feel emotionally overwhelmed in times of stress, that can cause them to shut down, stop, and procrastinate

Easy going, but they hate being controlled and will rebel. That is the line of their temper

Spiritual, connecting with nature and seeing the connection with all things

Tips for Nines

- Peace comes from solving your problems. Nines have a tendency to take the path of least resistance and avoid conflicts. This can make them resentful over time. It is important that nines learn to face their problems and work through them.

- Set strong boundaries. Nines may lose themselves attempting to keep the peace. It is important they set, and keep, strong personal boundaries, even in the face of possible conflict.

- Assert themselves. As the label "peacekeeper" implies, they will do a lot to maintain peace and order among the people around them, often by repressing their own thoughts and opinions. Nines must practice voicing their own thoughts and opinions, especially controversial ones.

Conclusion

"For those who believe, no proof is necessary. For those who don't believe, no proof is possible."

— Stuart Chase… or was it?

The quote also appears at the beginning of the popular 1943 film "The Song of Bernadette".

Father John LaFarge, a U.S. churchman, editor of The Catholic Weekly America, and member of a family noted in American arts, remarked about the miracles reported from Lourdes the appearance of the Holy Mother, Mary at Lourdes: "For those who believe in God no explanation is necessary. For those who do not believe in God no explanation is possible."

In March 1945 columnist James G. Stahlman of the "Nashville Banner" of Tennessee printed the following:

To the BELIEVER,

No explanation is necessary.

To the UNBELIEVER,

No explanation is possible.

It may be impossible to trace down the first time this wisdom was uttered. And so, it is with the Enneagram. We have seen how the same pool of knowledge was found in India, Egypt, Chaldea, and Greece, within Christian teachings and within the teachings of Islam, as well as other regions and religions of the world. Was it transmitted or re-discovered? Did Gurdjieff see these patterns repeated in the teaching of his Greek father, the Sufis, and throughout his travels? Did he borrow, synthesize, or build his system afresh? What about Ichazo and Naranjo? We know that Claudio Naranjo was of Arabic/Moorish, Spanish, and Jewish descent. Did he encounter the meaning of the types in his studies? We know he was considered a mystic and spiritual leader. He headed a global human potential movement and the spiritual renaissance of the late 20th century. Did he also use numerology or the teachings of Christian mystics as his base to expand the Enneagram?

We may never know what original sources were used. What we can be sure of is the sources we have investigated all have the same basic information in common, and when one reverses the types 5 and 7 in the Enneagram, we see an undeniable similarity between the personality types of numerology and the Enneagram. This leads one to believe these ancient sources were encountered and repurposed into the modern Enneagram.

The application of this knowledge is slightly different. Whereas the typing in numerology seeks the type by actions, the Enneagram seeks to type by underlying motivation.

Beyond this difference in approach and eliminating the pseudo-science of using a name or birthday to arrive at the type, there seems to be no great differences in the lines of delineation between the types within the two systems. However, if the reader does not wish to entertain the possibility that occult practice cannot carry in itself a scientific seed of truth, laying aside the math used in astrology, and the accidental discoveries that turned alchemy into chemistry, no explanation, obvious or not, will suffice.